STRENGTH *Renewed*

Learning to Wait on God

Pam Gillaspie

Strength Renewed: Learning to Wait on God

Copyright © 2026 by Pam Gillaspie
Published by Ignite Bible Ministries
www.pamgillaspie.com

ISBN 978-1-960938-31-2

Printed in the United States of America

2026

STRENGTH *Renewed*

Learning to Wait on God

Life happens. Whether it's family or church, job or kids, sickness or health, busyness or loneliness, life is filled with unpredictable elements, with variables that lift us up one day and come crashing down like waves over a ship's bow the next. Life happens.

In the midst of life happening, even the best intentions can run aground. Optimism says "Not me!" but we live in a broken world that both theologians and actuaries can tell you will eventually disappoint even the half-fulls among us.

Flexible inductive studies are designed with hopeful reality in mind! The main portion of the study offers flexibility to bend to each week's demands (and surprises!), and the Extra section at the end of each lesson invites those with different learning styles—and the occasional gift of more time—to try some new ways of remembering the lesson.

When life happens, don't drop your Bible . . . hold it more tightly and flex!

Enjoy!

How to use this study

Flexible Inductive Studies meet you where you are and take you as far as you want to go.

1. **WEEKLY LESSON:** The main text guides you through the complete topic of study for the week.

2. **FYI:** The For Your Information boxes provide bite-sized material to shed additional light on the topic.

3. **ONE STEP FURTHER:** One Step Further sections included in some lessons give you the option to push yourself a little further. These boxes give you the ultimate in flexibility.

4. **DIGGING DEEPER:** If you're looking to go further, Digging Deeper sections will help you sharpen your skills as you continue to mine the truths of Scripture for yourself.

5. **EXTRA:** This is strictly bonus material to help you think through what you've learned from a little different angle.

Contents

Are You Weary?

> *" . . . those who wait for the LORD will gain*
> *new strength . . ."*
> —Isaiah 40:31a

It seems that today everyone is weary from something. The pace of life in the world, in *your* world, is frenetic! You know it. I know it. Going here and driving there, we're trying to keep our lives and our families on track in a world full of busyness, distractions, and every kind of opportunity.

The tools designed to make life easier have struck back like the other side of a double-edged sword. As we do more things more quickly, instead of increasing downtime, we face increasing quotas. As download speeds increase and as AI puts more curated data at our fingertips, our output capacity continues to be stretched—sometimes to failure. You know exactly what I mean, don't you? Most of us are weary as our capacity is challenged and stretched each . . . and every . . . day.

FYI:

If You're in a Class

Work on **Lesson One** together on your first day of class. This will be a great way to start getting to know each other and to be able to start right away by encouraging one another in the faith as Hebrews 3:13 exhorts: "But encourage one another day after day, as long as it is still called 'Today,' so that none of you will be hardened by the deceitfulness of sin."

During the COVID years, we learned that weariness wears different outfits. Even when our world ground to a stop during the pandemic, weariness hung around. We no longer hustled from place to place, but we wearied nonetheless from the interruption and abnormality of life.

Oddly, during those strange days, we wearied of not being able to do the very things that we thought were the root causes of our weariness in the first place, and we learned that the paths to weariness are many and varied.

WEARINESS IS NOT A BADGE OF HONOR

We're often inclined to think that weariness born out of hard work and exertion should earn us, if nothing else, the undying thanks of those who've "caused" it—be they needy children or an overbearing boss—of those we've labored over (and over and over in some cases!) to the point of exhaustion. If we're honest, sometimes we even think our weariness pleases God. After all, doesn't it show just how hard we're trying?

"Weary," though, is not a badge of honor. In fact, it's something we're *warned* about in the Bible . . . and the cure may be different than what you'd think!

WHERE ARE YOU TODAY?

Are you weary? Have you been weary? Do you know others who are weary? Explain.

What do you typically do when you feel weary? Do you sleep? Watch some form of media? Eat? Do something else?

Do you move toward or away from people when you're weary? With what result?

What weariness are you carrying today? What typically wearies you?

Have you learned to see weariness coming or does it tend to blind side you?

BIBLICAL WORDS ON WEARINESS

Sometimes we're just plain tired and need to rest or go to sleep. John tells his readers that when Jesus met the woman at the well, He was weary from His journey (John 4:6). That kind of weary happens. Sleep it off and you're good in the morning.

There's another weariness—we might call it a weariness of soul—that Paul talks about in Galatians when he tells his readers to "not grow weary of doing good" (ESV). Maybe you're there; sometimes I am. Perhaps we won't verbalize it and maybe we won't even let ourselves think about it because we're afraid. We have *worked* so hard and so long and we are tired. Sometimes it's that we've *waited* so long and so patiently and, again, we are exhausted. Some days we want to give up. If that's you today, know for certain that you are not alone and that there is an answer. God Himself freely offers the strength we lack.

Before we look at what Paul says in Galatians 6:9-10, let's put his words in the greater context of his letter to the churches of Galatia. As you may already know, Paul wrote Galatians as a defense of the true Gospel in the face of a false gospel of works righteousness that had infiltrated the churches of the region.

Jewish believers in Jesus were falling back into Judaism and trying to take Gentile believers along with them back to the Law. They had a "Jesus+" theology. In dispelling this aberrant teaching, Paul reminds the Galatians of their adoption as sons of God, of their freedom from the slavery of sin, and their power for righteous living because of the indwelling Holy Spirit. All of this has resulted from their identification with Christ, having been crucified with Him (Galatians 2:20).

It's easy to read over the verses as just another exhortation in a New Testament letter, but think for a moment of the example of Paul's own life. He is all-in on the Gospel of Jesus Christ—he knows what it is to be persecuted, beaten, and chased out of town after town because of his stand for the Gospel. Eventually he will die for it. The Galatians, though, instead of clinging to the truth and standing boldly with Paul are nibbling at the edges of heresy and becoming one more entry on a list that Paul has to deal with and correct. They, themselves, provided him a ripe opportunity to grow weary in doing good! Sometimes I tire just reading about them.

Life in a broken and fallen world is challenging even with the indwelling Holy Spirt. John warns about loving the world and its lust of the flesh, lust of the eyes, and boastful pride (1 John 2:15-16). Peter reminds us that our adversary prowls like a lion seeking someone to devour, literally seeking someone to swallow (1 Peter 5:8). Each of these fits the category of clear and present danger. But weariness? Not so much.

Weariness sneaks up from behind and strikes from the shadows. Many of us live as resident aliens in its land without even realizing it! It is fitting then, that as he finishes his letter Paul exhorts his readers with these words: "Let us not lose heart in doing good, for in due time we will reap if we do not grow weary. So then, while we have opportunity, let us do good to all people, and especially to those who are of the household of the faith" (Galatians 6:9-10).

We're going to look at these two verses inductively, asking questions of the text so we don't read past or read over truth that can challenge us and change us.

LET'S EXPLORE!

While some of us like to study, I know that others consider "study" to be a five-letter, four-letter word. Because of that, I'd like to encourage you to think a little differently about what we're doing as we look at the texts of Scripture. Simply ask questions and notice connections. Pay attention to repetitions, to comparisons, and to contrasts. Just be inquisitive! I'm going to prompt you with some questions, but don't feel like you have to stop there.

Think of the last time you went on a major Google hunt to find *that* information on whatever *it was* you had to uncover—the deal, the scoop, the first release—whatever it was, tap into your inner journalist, hunter, or general snoop and let's get at it!

How do I mark?
Circle, box, underline, colored pencil . . . you can have fun with this. This is one of those places where there is no "right" and no "wrong." Be as creative (or uncreative!) as you want. The marking is simply to help you slow down and better observe elements in the text.

Let's Start by Marking

Nothing fancy here, just mark the following in distinct ways to help you as you observe and explore:

- the phrases *doing good* and *do good*
- phrases beginning with *not*
- the two phrases that refer to time

Galatians 6:9-10

9 *Let us not lose heart in doing good, for in due time we will reap if we do not grow weary.*

10 *So then, while we have opportunity, let us do good to all people, and especially to those who are of the household of the faith.*

> **GALATIANS 6:9-10**
>
> 9   Let us not lose heart in doing good, for in due time we will reap if we do not grow weary.
>
> 10 So then, while we have opportunity, let us do good to all people, and especially to those who are of the household of the faith.

Let's Ask Some Questions

What does Paul *not* want his readers to do? What are the two ways he says it?

What are some ways you are prone to lose heart or grow weary in doing good?

What collateral damage happens when we grow weary in this way?

What encouragement does Paul give for the future?

How can this future hope help us in the here and now?

What happens when we lack hope? Can you think of a time when you lost hope in someone or something? What happened? How did it affect you and others?

What positive exhortation or encouragement does Paul give the Galatians?

What are some specific ways you do this with "all people"? How has this changed during different seasons of your life?

ONE STEP FURTHER

Kairos and Chronos

Two Greek words are often translated into English as *time: kairos* and *chronos.* In Galatians 6:9-10, *kairos* appears twice. Once it is translated as *time,* the other as *opportunity.* If you have a few extra minutes this week, see what you can discover about how *kairos* time differs from *chronos* time!

How have people responded to you when you have sought to do good to them? Explain.

What are ways you can do good to those who are of the "household of faith"? How have others in the household of faith done good to you?

What does "opportunity" (Greek: *kairos*, literally "season" or "time") have to do with this?

What tensions do these verses leave you with? What wisdom will you need to obey?

DOES MARKING REALLY HELP?

I know. Some of you don't like the idea of marking. I get that and there is no Bible study law that says you have to . . . although you may have run into a well-meaning person who has told you otherwise. Before we close out this week, I want to show you simply how to see some of the elements more clearly. Please know that this is not the *right* way to do it. This is *one way* that helps me to see the elements better.

Again, this is just an example. You may decide to write the verses out and emphasize the "let us" and "let us not" phrases. You may key in on the "if / then" component. These are all different elements of looking closely at the Word, of turning the gem of Scripture and seeing it sparkle from different angles.

On the following pages, I'll show you how you can simply mark the 5 Ws and H by boldfacing one element at a time. I've also put implied words in brackets and aligned a short list that is in the text.

Who?   Mark people and the pronouns referring to them.

What?   Mark the main topic.

When?   Mark phrases related to time or sequencing.

Where?   Mark location words (none in this example).

Why?   Mark words related to purpose.

How?   Mark words that modify the main topic.

Galatians 6:9-10 — *Who?*
(Mark people and the pronouns referring to them.)

9 Let **us** not lose heart in doing good,

for in due time **we** will reap

if **we** do not grow weary [in doing good].

10 So then, while **we** have opportunity,

let **us** do good to   (1) **all people,**

and especially

[let **us** do good]* to (2) **those who are of the household of the faith.**

***Note:** The bracketed words are implied. I'm putting them in so you can better visualize the structure of the verses.

Galatians 6:9-10 — <u>What?</u>
(Mark words that show the main topic.)

9 Let us not lose heart in **<u>doing good,</u>**

for in due time we will reap

if we do not grow weary [in doing good].

10 So then, while we have opportunity,

let us **<u>do good</u>** to   (1) all people,

and especially

[let us do good] to   (2) those who are of the household of the

faith.

Galatians 6:9-10 — <u>When?</u>
(Mark phrases related to time.)

9 Let us not lose heart in doing good,

for **<u>in due time</u>** we will reap

if we do not grow weary [in doing good].

10 So then, **<u>while we have opportunity</u>**,

let us do good to   (1) all people,

and especially

[let us do good] to   (2) those who are of the household of the

faith.

Galatians 6:9-10 — _Why?_
(Mark words related to purpose.)

9 Let us not lose heart in doing good,

for in due time **we will reap**

if we do not grow weary [in doing good].

10 So then, while we have opportunity,

let us do good to   (1) all people,

and especially

[let us do good] to   (2) those who are of the household of the

faith.

Galatians 6:9-10 — _How?_
(Mark words that modify the main topic.)

9 Let us **not lose heart** in doing good,

for in due time we will reap

if we do **not grow weary** [in doing good].

10 So then, while we have opportunity,

let us do good to   (1) all people,

and especially

[let us do good] to   (2) those who are of the household of the

faith.

EXTRA

This is strictly bonus material. Some are activities meant to help combat weariness, while others may help you think about what you've learned from a little different angle.

Leisure Reading

Spend some time leisurely reading the Bible this week. Pick a book and stick with it; don't just hunt and peck topically. Jot down your biggest takeaways from it.

Intentional Encouragement

Reach out to someone this week and encourage that person in the Lord. It can be via email, text, phone call, Zoom, or in person. Write down who you reached out to.

Leisure Listening

Really busy? Take some time to listen to the Word while you're in the car, making dinner, shoveling snow, folding laundry. Jot down below what you listened to!

Memorize Key Verses

Why not try that out this week and commit Galatians 6:9-10 to memory? When you've got it, see if you can write it below without peeking!

#Hashtag It

Make a hashtag for Galatians 6:9-10.

"Post" It

Brevity can make us think more accurately. See if you can summarize what you've learned this week in 280 characters or less.

Now take 280 more characters to summarize how you're applying what you've learned!

Lesson Two

A Cautionary Tale

"The thing that you are doing is not good. You will surely wear out, both yourself and these people who are with you, for the task is too heavy for you; you cannot do it alone."
—Exodus 18:18

The Bible is clear that *growing weary* and *losing heart* are related. We know it, too, don't we? We know it in the core of our souls because as human beings we know we have limits. We hate it, but we know it. Yes, the Holy Spirit empowers believers so we don't have to stumble along in the flesh, but there are only so many hours in a day and only so many days in a week. There are only so many years in a lifetime. To fight against capacity is to try to kick the bottom out of a glass jar. You may be able to do it, but with what result?

Much of our culture wars against this. In fact, one "truth" it propagates is this: "If you're not tired, you're not working; if you're not worn out, you're lazy." Seriously, how much Pinterest shaming can any one person tolerate? Really. Instead of paying attention to weariness as a warning, many of us have worn it as a badge. I've got an old Caribou Coffee t-shirt that brags "You can sleep when you're dead!"

Perhaps you're wonderfully balanced and well-adjusted! Maybe you're busy from time to time but you've never looked burnout in the eyes. Maybe the people never, ever get to *you.* Maybe you've even thought: "That would never be me!"—it's what I used to think. It's probably what Moses and Elijah would have said, too! "When I'm doing God's work, how could I become weary in doing good?"

Don't Forget to Pray
Ask God to help you focus, understand, enjoy, and apply His Word!

WHERE ARE YOU TODAY?

Has anyone ever warned you about something? If so, what was the context?

How did you respond?

WARNING REJECTED

Perhaps I'm duller than average or maybe there's more arrogance in my fiber than I care to admit. Whatever the reason, I rejected a warning about being too busy when I was in my early thirties and learned a lesson that I'll never forget. A person close to me, wiser than me, and who had my best intentions at heart told me in no uncertain terms that I was overbooked and headed for trouble.

Being young and invincible I smiled, nodded, rejected truth, and marched at a quickened pace toward burnout. By the grace of God those wise words woke me up from my breakneck stupor before I crashed and burned, but not before I got a good look at weariness firsthand.

Perhaps you've had a near miss, too. Perhaps you're sitting in the middle of burnout today and this study is a chance to reexamine what is important in life and what isn't.

This week, we're going to look at one of my favorite accounts from the Bible that tells us about a time in Moses' life when he was an eyelash away from growing weary and losing heart himself before his father-in-law warned him about the danger of shouldering too heavy a burden. Let's take a look for ourselves.

A LOOK AT THE LIFE OF MOSES

As we pick up the story, we find Moses with the children of Israel. The people have recently been delivered out of Egyptian captivity where they have been slaves for the better part of 430 years. The young nation has also weathered its first-ever battle fighting off attackers in the wilderness with rookie "soldiers" who have only known slavery.

By now the people have also shown their true colors—grumbling for water and food—but God their Deliverer has shown Himself ever faithful to both guide and provide.

As we come to the scene, Moses' father-in-law is bringing his wife and sons back to him. They had accompanied Moses to Egypt (see Exodus 4), but at some point during the Egyptian adventure he had sent them back to her father in the land of Midian.

LET'S EXPLORE!

As we begin exploring this critical interaction between Moses and his father-in-law, we'll need the context from **Exodus 18.** It's always good to read the text from your Bible, but we'll include it here, too, so you can feel more free to mark it up. Context keeps us grounded in what God is actually saying in His Word. If we start picking out pieces here and there without paying attention to their surroundings, the likelihood that we will misinterpret rises dramatically.

Let's Read

Exodus 18

1   *Now Jethro, the priest of Midian, Moses' father-in-law, heard of all that God had done for Moses and for Israel His people, how the LORD had brought Israel out of Egypt.*

2   *Jethro, Moses' father-in-law, took Moses' wife Zipporah, after he had sent her away,*

3   *and her two sons, of whom one was named Gershom, for Moses said, "I have been a sojourner in a foreign land."*

4   *The other was named Eliezer, for he said, "The God of my father was my help, and delivered me from the sword of Pharaoh."*

5   *Then Jethro, Moses' father-in-law, came with his sons and his wife to Moses in the wilderness where he was camped, at the mount of God.*

6   *He sent word to Moses, "I, your father-in-law Jethro, am coming to you with your wife and her two sons with her."*

7   *Then Moses went out to meet his father-in-law, and he bowed down and kissed him; and they asked each other of their welfare and went into the tent.*

8   *Moses told his father-in-law all that the LORD had done to Pharaoh and to the Egyptians for Israel's sake, all the hardship that had befallen them on the journey, and how the LORD had delivered them.*

9   *Jethro rejoiced over all the goodness which the LORD had done to Israel, in delivering them from the hand of the Egyptians.*

10   So Jethro said, "Blessed be the LORD who delivered you from the hand of the Egyptians and from the hand of Pharaoh, and who delivered the people from under the hand of the Egyptians.

11   "Now I know that the LORD is greater than all the gods; indeed, it was proven when they dealt proudly against the people."

12   Then Jethro, Moses' father-in-law, took a burnt offering and sacrifices for God, and Aaron came with all the elders of Israel to eat a meal with Moses' father-in-law before God.

13   It came about the next day that Moses sat to judge the people, and the people stood about Moses from the morning until the evening.

14   Now when Moses' father-in-law saw all that he was doing for the people, he said, "What is this thing that you are doing for the people? Why do you alone sit as judge and all the people stand about you from morning until evening?"

15   Moses said to his father-in-law, "Because the people come to me to inquire of God.

16   "When they have a dispute, it comes to me, and I judge between a man and his neighbor and make known the statutes of God and His laws."

17   Moses' father-in-law said to him, "The thing that you are doing is not good.

18   "You will surely wear out, both yourself and these people who are with you, for the task is too heavy for you; you cannot do it alone.

19 *"Now listen to me: I will give you counsel, and God be with you. You be the people's representative before God, and you bring the disputes to God,*

20 *then teach them the statutes and the laws, and make known to them the way in which they are to walk and the work they are to do.*

21 *"Furthermore, you shall select out of all the people able men who fear God, men of truth, those who hate dishonest gain; and you shall place these over them as leaders of thousands, of hundreds, of fifties and of tens.*

22 *"Let them judge the people at all times; and let it be that every major dispute they will bring to you, but every minor dispute they themselves will judge. So it will be easier for you, and they will bear the burden with you.*

23 *"If you do this thing and God so commands you, then you will be able to endure, and all these people also will go to their place in peace."*

24 *So Moses listened to his father-in-law and did all that he had said.*

25 *Moses chose able men out of all Israel and made them heads over the people, leaders of thousands, of hundreds, of fifties and of tens.*

26 *They judged the people at all times; the difficult dispute they would bring to Moses, but every minor dispute they themselves would judge.*

27 *Then Moses bade his father-in-law farewell, and he went his way into his own land.*

Let's Start by Marking

Now that we have the context, let's focus our attention on verses 13-16 and do some marking together. Again, this will help us slow down and pay closer attention. Let's mark:

- references to *Moses* (including pronouns)
- time phrases

Exodus 18:13-16

13 It came about the next day that Moses sat to judge the people, and the people stood about Moses from the morning until the evening.

14 Now when Moses' father-in-law saw all that he was doing for the people, he said, "What is this thing that you are doing for the people? Why do you alone sit as judge and all the people stand about you from morning until evening?"

15 Moses said to his father-in-law, "Because the people come to me to inquire of God.

16 "When they have a dispute, it comes to me, and I judge between a man and his neighbor and make known the statutes of God and His laws."

Let's Ask Some Questions

What was Moses doing? Do you think the activity itself was a good one? Why or why not?

How much of his time did it take?

Have you had (or do you have?!) something that monopolizes your "morning until evening"? If so, what is it?

What effect is it having on you? On your family?

What kind of pressure was Moses under that caused him to go "morning until evening"? Was it a God-given assignment or something else?

How do you determine if something in your life is a God-given assignment or not? What difference does figuring this out make?

How much do you allow other people to determine how you spend or invest your time?

What should be the deciding factor on your use of your time? Why?

Let's Mark

Let's continue with the next two verses and mark:

- references to Moses' work (*the thing, the task*)

Exodus 18:17-18

17 *Moses' father-in-law said to him, "The thing that you are doing is*
    not good.

18 *"You will surely wear out, both yourself and these people who are*
    with you, for the task is too heavy for you; you cannot do it alone.

Let's Ask Some Questions

What two statements does Moses' father-in-law, Jethro, make about
Moses' work?

What is it that Jethro thinks Moses isn't doing well? What does he say will
result?

What factors add up to this being a bad situation for Moses and the
people?

If Jethro knocked on your door tomorrow, do you think there's anything in your life that he'd say is going to wear you out? If so, what?

Don't worry, we'll be thinking about application soon!

NABAL, NABAL

When Jethro tells Moses that he will "surely wear out," he uses the Hebrew **nabel** twice. In a sense it is an unremarkable word that means to wear out, crumble, fade, or wither. We see it in Isaiah 40:7-8 where it is twice translated *fades*:

> "The grass withers, the flower **fades** [Hebrew: **nabel**],
>
> When the breath of the LORD blows upon it;
>
> Surely the people are grass.
>
> The grass withers, the flower **fades** [Hebrew: **nabel**],
>
> But the word of our God stands forever."

What is interesting, though, is that the root of this word in Hebrew is NBL, the same as for the word *foolish.* Perhaps you'll remember the account of David's wife Abigail who prior to marrying him was the wife of Nabal whose name meant "foolish" (1 Samuel 25).

While the context of Exodus certainly supports the "wear out" translation and Jethro does not accuse Moses of foolishness, the root reminds us of the need for wisdom in our actions.

Suffice it to say that pushing ourselves to burn out, break down, or wear out is simply not wise. Moses was God's chosen leader but he still needed instruction from his father-in-law to keep him from pressing on down a well-intentioned but unwise and dangerous road.

THINKING ABOUT THE REST OF THE STORY . . .

Re-read the account of Moses and Jethro in Exodus 18 and then consider the following questions.

What does Jethro counsel Moses to do?

How does Moses respond to Jethro's intervention?

Why do you think he responded so well?

What did you learn this week about weariness in Moses' life that you can apply in the situations of your life?

EXTRA

Remember, this is bonus material to encourage and equip you, not to burden or weary you.

Leisure Reading or Listening

Keep up your leisure reading of God's Word! Jot down what you've been reading and your biggest takeaways. Then share with someone else what you've been learning and applying.

Intentional Encouragement

Did you skip this last week? Reach out to someone this week and encourage that person in the Lord. Write down who you reached out to and how it was received.

Memorize Key Verses

Pick a key verse from Exodus 18, write it below, and commit it to memory.

#Hashtag It

Make a hashtag for Exodus 18.

"Post" It

Summarize what you've learned this week in 280 characters or less.

Now take 280 more characters to summarize how you're applying what you've learned!

Lesson Three

You Are Not Alone!

"I have been very zealous for the LORD, the God of hosts;
for the sons of Israel have forsaken Your covenant, torn
down Your altars and killed Your prophets with the sword.
And I alone am left;
and they seek my life, to take it away."
—1 Kings 19:10

The prophet Elijah scored one of the biggest wins in all of the Old Testament. Working against staggering odds, but empowered by God's strength, Elijah purged hundreds of prophets of the false god Baal from Israel. He witnessed God's strength and power for life firsthand. Firsthand. Can you imagine? As we look at his story, you may find yourself thinking that if God came through like that for you, you'd never have a weary worry again! The reality of God's power is a game-changer. Still, *do we know it, and will we live in light of it and in submission to Him?*

WHERE ARE YOU TODAY?

Have you ever felt like you were totally alone in a situation? If so, what was the situation and what were the emotions?

Are you there today?

How do you think isolation or feelings of loneliness affects weariness?

"I ALONE AM LEFT"

In our last lesson, we saw that Moses couldn't bear the weight of the Israelites alone. He needed help. He needed others alongside him. While purposely making time to be alone with God yields great gain (think Jacob wrestling with God, think Moses on the mountain with God, think Jesus withdrawing before the sun would rise to pray), "alone" is not how God created man to be.

Think back with me to the book of Genesis. After God created the world and deemed "all that He had made" as "very good," He said that it was not good for the man to be alone (Genesis 1:31, 2:18). Interestingly, the word translated "alone" comes from the Hebrew word *bad* meaning alone, apart from others, or by oneself. While unrelated to the English word "bad," it is a memorable coincidence. Throughout the Word we see God's people in community—from the children of Israel in the Old Testament to those in the New Testament and beyond (including us!) who are part of the Church and grafted in to God's people!

Today, we're going to look at an account from the life of Elijah who, after a stunning victory, fell headlong into the pit of despair largely because he saw himself as being alone. While his story may have some flashier details than yours or mine, it is rooted in common fears and a common human response to the sensation of being alone in difficult times.

A LOOK AT THE LIFE OF ELIJAH

As we pick up the story, King Ahab is in the midst of his 22-year reign over the northern kingdom of Israel. It's an easy number to read over, but imagine for a moment coming to the end of eight years of an incumbent president and there being no chance to vote him out. Ahab ruled for the American equivalent of five-and-a-half terms with no hope of removing him along the way, short of a coup or civil war. When Elijah encounters Ahab's false prophets at Mount Carmel in 1 Kings 16, Ahab is likely 17 or so years into his reign of evil and terror.

Ahab wasn't just a little bit evil. No. His evil was unprecedented. According to 1 Kings 16:30-33, Ahab did *more evil* in the sight of the LORD than *any* of the kings before him. He married an evil wife named Jezebel from an idol-worshipping country and then worshiped idols himself. He also promoted idol worship in Israel. Verse 33 sums up his life when it says, "Thus Ahab did more to provoke the LORD God of Israel than all the kings of Israel who were before him." What a twisted legacy.

ONE STEP FURTHER

"Don'ts" That Ahab Did

If you want to see for yourself how blatantly Ahab disobeyed God's clear commands to His people, read Deuteronomy 7:1-5 and jot down below what you learn.

LET'S EXPLORE!

The account of Elijah's interactions with Ahab is recorded in 1 Kings 17, 18, and 19. One of the historical books of the Bible, 1 Kings records the history of the kings of Israel and Judah—from the end of the life of David who was king over both Israel and Judah up to the time when Jehoshaphat ruled in Judah and Ahaziah, the son of Ahab, ruled in Israel.

We'll include the text here for convenience, but always feel free to read or listen in your own Bible. After answering some basic questions on the text, we'll focus on marking some specific verses together.

Let's Read

1 Kings 17

1 *Now Elijah the Tishbite, who was of the settlers of Gilead, said to Ahab, "As the LORD, the God of Israel lives, before whom I stand, surely there shall be neither dew nor rain these years, except by my word."*

2 *The word of the LORD came to him, saying,*

3 *"Go away from here and turn eastward, and hide yourself by the brook Cherith, which is east of the Jordan.*

4 *"It shall be that you will drink of the brook, and I have commanded the ravens to provide for you there."*

5 *So he went and did according to the word of the LORD, for he went and lived by the brook Cherith, which is east of the Jordan.*

6 *The ravens brought him bread and meat in the morning and bread and meat in the evening, and he would drink from the brook.*

7 *It happened after a while that the brook dried up, because there was no rain in the land.*

James' Commentary on Elijah

"The effective prayer of a righteous man can accomplish much. Elijah was a man with a nature like ours, and he prayed earnestly that it would not rain, and it did not rain on earth for three years and six months. Then he prayed again, and the sky poured rain and the earth produced its fruit."

—James 5:16b-18

8 Then the word of the LORD came to him, saying,

9 "Arise, go to Zarephath, which belongs to Sidon, and stay there; behold, I have commanded a widow there to provide for you."

10 So he arose and went to Zarephath, and when he came to the gate of the city, behold, a widow was there gathering sticks; and he called to her and said, "Please get me a little water in a jar, that I may drink."

11 As she was going to get it, he called to her and said, "Please bring me a piece of bread in your hand."

12 But she said, "As the LORD your God lives, I have no bread, only a handful of flour in the bowl and a little oil in the jar; and behold, I am gathering a few sticks that I may go in and prepare for me and my son, that we may eat it and die."

13 Then Elijah said to her, "Do not fear; go, do as you have said, but make me a little bread cake from it first and bring it out to me, and afterward you may make one for yourself and for your son.

14 "For thus says the LORD God of Israel, 'The bowl of flour shall not be exhausted, nor shall the jar of oil be empty, until the day that the LORD sends rain on the face of the earth.' "

15 So she went and did according to the word of Elijah, and she and he and her household ate for many days.

16 *The bowl of flour was not exhausted nor did the jar of oil become empty, according to the word of the LORD which He spoke through Elijah.*

17 *Now it came about after these things that the son of the woman, the mistress of the house, became sick; and his sickness was so severe that there was no breath left in him.*

18 *So she said to Elijah, "What do I have to do with you, O man of God? You have come to me to bring my iniquity to remembrance and to put my son to death!"*

19 *He said to her, "Give me your son." Then he took him from her bosom and carried him up to the upper room where he was living, and laid him on his own bed.*

20 *He called to the LORD and said, "O LORD my God, have You also brought calamity to the widow with whom I am staying, by causing her son to die?"*

21 *Then he stretched himself upon the child three times, and called to the Lord and said, "O LORD my God, I pray You, let this child's life return to him."*

22 *The LORD heard the voice of Elijah, and the life of the child returned to him and he revived.*

23 *Elijah took the child and brought him down from the upper room into the house and gave him to his mother; and Elijah said, "See, your son is alive."*

24 *Then the woman said to Elijah, "Now I know that you are a man of God and that the word of the LORD in your mouth is truth."*

Let's Ask Some Questions

(based on **1 Kings 17**)

What bad news does Elijah bring to King Ahab? What challenges will this mean for all of the people, including Elijah?

What other potential danger will Elijah face after bringing this message to King Ahab?

One question that may have come to your mind in reading 1 Kings 17 is "Did a mere man actually stop the rain?" It's a good question. Only God stops and starts the rain, right? Yes, God controls the rain, *and* He also ties it to covenantal obedience in Deuteronomy. This covenant that the people of Israel willingly entered into with God involved blessings and curses. If the people followed God, He promised to bless them abundantly; if they turned away in disobedience, they would bring curses upon themselves.

Obedience and rain were bound together, which posed a major problem for a country following a godless king (check it out for yourself in Deuteronomy 28:15, 23-24). It was during the time of godless King Ahab that Elijah prayed for God to stop the rain. James tells us that God heard this righteous man's prayer and the rain stopped.

While we may be getting a little ahead of the story here, do note that Ahab and his idol-worshiping wife Jezebel are live threats to Elijah's health and well-being. We'll see clear evidence of this in 1 Kings 18. Before we get there, though, let's take a look at how God specifically cares for Elijah during this tumultuous time.

Let's Do Some Marking

Since you've already read 1 Kings 17, let's look more closely at God's specific directions to Elijah and His provision for him. In the verses that follow, mark:

- the specific instructions God gives to Elijah
- the phrases that begin with "I have commanded . . ."

1 Kings 17:2-4, 8-9

2 *The word of the LORD came to him, saying,*

3 *"Go away from here and turn eastward, and hide yourself by the brook Cherith, which is east of the Jordan.*

4 *"It shall be that you will drink of the brook, and I have commanded the ravens to provide for you there."*

8 *Then the word of the LORD came to him, saying,*

9 *"Arise, go to Zarephath, which belongs to Sidon, and stay there; behold, I have commanded a widow there to provide for you."*

Let's Ask Some More Questions

What phrase indicates that God is talking to Elijah?

What two instructions does God give Elijah in verse 3? Based on the context, why do you think God said this to him?

What will God do for Elijah? Who will He command to get that job done?

What does this show about God's concern for Elijah and His power to care for him?

What two instructions does the LORD give to Elijah in verse 9 after the brook Cherith dries up?

Who does God command to provide for Elijah this time?

If you were Elijah, how do you think your faith would have been impacted by being fed by unclean birds and then by a foreign, starving widow?

Have any events in your life caused you to wonder how God would provide?

How have you seen God provide in your life? Think both in terms of write-it-down-so-I-don't-forget provision and everyday provision.

At first glance, the fact that God provided for Elijah by way of birds seems more amazing than providing by a person. When you think twice, though, God didn't command just any person to feed Elijah—He commanded a woman, a foreigner, a widow with a child who was starving to death. Provision by the birds was a miracle, but provision by the widow was even more!

By birds and by a widow, God has kept Elijah safe, alive, and well fed. Elijah has faced challenges during the famine and drought, but God has shown Himself more than adequate to care and provide for whatever the prophet will need.

Let's Read Again

Now that we've considered some of the implications of God's provision for Elijah in 1 Kings 17, let's read 1 Kings 18 and move on to some more questions. Do note that 1 Kings 18 takes place three years after the events of the previous chapter.

1 Kings 18

1   *Now it happened* after *many days that the word of the LORD came to Elijah in the third year, saying, "Go, show yourself to Ahab, and I will send rain on the face of the earth."*

2   *So Elijah went to show himself to Ahab. Now the famine* was *severe in Samaria.*

3   *Ahab called Obadiah who was over the household. (Now Obadiah feared the LORD greatly;*

4   *for when Jezebel destroyed the prophets of the LORD, Obadiah took a hundred prophets and hid them by fifties in a cave, and provided them with bread and water.)*

5   *Then Ahab said to Obadiah, "Go through the land to all the springs of water and to all the valleys; perhaps we will find grass and keep the horses and mules alive, and not have to kill some of the cattle."*

6   *So they divided the land between them to survey it; Ahab went one way by himself and Obadiah went another way by himself.*

7 *Now as Obadiah was on the way, behold, Elijah met him, and he recognized him and fell on his face and said, "Is this you, Elijah my master?"*

8 *He said to him, "It is I. Go, say to your master, 'Behold, Elijah is here.' "*

9 *He said, "What sin have I committed, that you are giving your servant into the hand of Ahab to put me to death?*

10 *"As the LORD your God lives, there is no nation or kingdom where my master has not sent to search for you; and when they said, 'He is not here,' he made the kingdom or nation swear that they could not find you.*

11 *"And now you are saying, 'Go, say to your master, "Behold, Elijah is here." '*

12 *"It will come about when I leave you that the Spirit of the LORD will carry you where I do not know; so when I come and tell Ahab and he cannot find you, he will kill me, although I your servant have feared the LORD from my youth.*

13 *"Has it not been told to my master what I did when Jezebel killed the prophets of the LORD, that I hid a hundred prophets of the LORD by fifties in a cave, and provided them with bread and water?*

14 *"And now you are saying, 'Go, say to your master, "Behold, Elijah is here" '; he will then kill me."*

15 *Elijah said, "As the LORD of hosts lives, before whom I stand, I will surely show myself to him today."*

16 *So Obadiah went to meet Ahab and told him; and Ahab went to meet Elijah.*

17 When Ahab saw Elijah, Ahab said to him, "Is this you, you troubler
    of Israel?"

18 He said, "I have not troubled Israel, but you and your father's house
    have, because you have forsaken the commandments of the LORD
    and you have followed the Baals.

19 "Now then send and gather to me all Israel at Mount Carmel,
    together with 450 prophets of Baal and 400 prophets of the
    Asherah, who eat at Jezebel's table."

20 So Ahab sent a message among all the sons of Israel and brought
    the prophets together at Mount Carmel.

21 Elijah came near to all the people and said, "How long will you
    hesitate between two opinions? If the LORD is God, follow Him; but
    if Baal, follow him." But the people did not answer him a word.

22 Then Elijah said to the people, "I alone am left a prophet of the
    LORD, but Baal's prophets are 450 men.

23 "Now let them give us two oxen; and let them choose one ox for
    themselves and cut it up, and place it on the wood, but put no fire
    under it; and I will prepare the other ox and lay it on the wood, and
    I will not put a fire under it.

24 "Then you call on the name of your god, and I will call on the name
    of the Lord, and the God who answers by fire, He is God." And all
    the people said, "That is a good idea."

25 So Elijah said to the prophets of Baal, "Choose one ox for yourselves
    and prepare it first for you are many, and call on the name of your
    god, but put no fire under it."

26 *Then they took the ox which was given them and they prepared it and called on the name of Baal from morning until noon saying, "O Baal, answer us." But there was no voice and no one answered. And they leaped about the altar which they made.*

27 *It came about at noon, that Elijah mocked them and said, "Call out with a loud voice, for he is a god; either he is occupied or gone aside, or is on a journey, or perhaps he is asleep and needs to be awakened."*

28 *So they cried with a loud voice and cut themselves according to their custom with swords and lances until the blood gushed out on them.*

29 *When midday was past, they raved until the time of the offering of the evening sacrifice; but there was no voice, no one answered, and no one paid attention.*

30 *Then Elijah said to all the people, "Come near to me." So all the people came near to him. And he repaired the altar of the Lord which had been torn down.*

31 *Elijah took twelve stones according to the number of the tribes of the sons of Jacob, to whom the word of the Lord had come, saying, "Israel shall be your name."*

32 *So with the stones he built an altar in the name of the Lord, and he made a trench around the altar, large enough to hold two measures of seed.*

33 *Then he arranged the wood and cut the ox in pieces and laid it on the wood.*

34 And he said, "Fill four pitchers with water and pour it on the burnt offering and on the wood." And he said, "Do it a second time," and they did it a second time. And he said, "Do it a third time," and they did it a third time.

35 The water flowed around the altar and he also filled the trench with water.

36 At the time of the offering of the evening sacrifice, Elijah the prophet came near and said, "O LORD, the God of Abraham, Isaac and Israel, today let it be known that You are God in Israel and that I am Your servant and I have done all these things at Your word.

37 "Answer me, O LORD, answer me, that this people may know that You, O LORD, are God, and that You have turned their heart back again."

38 Then the fire of the LORD fell and consumed the burnt offering and the wood and the stones and the dust, and licked up the water that was in the trench.

39 When all the people saw it, they fell on their faces; and they said, "The LORD, He is God; the Lord, He is God."

40 Then Elijah said to them, "Seize the prophets of Baal; do not let one of them escape." So they seized them; and Elijah brought them down to the brook Kishon, and slew them there.

41 *Now Elijah said to Ahab, "Go up, eat and drink; for there is the sound of the roar of a heavy shower."*

42 *So Ahab went up to eat and drink. But Elijah went up to the top of Carmel; and he crouched down on the earth and put his face between his knees.*

43 *He said to his servant, "Go up now, look toward the sea." So he went up and looked and said, "There is nothing." And he said, "Go back" seven times.*

44 *It came about at the seventh time, that he said, "Behold, a cloud as small as a man's hand is coming up from the sea." And he said, "Go up, say to Ahab, 'Prepare your chariot and go down, so that the heavy shower does not stop you.' "*

45 *In a little while the sky grew black with clouds and wind, and there was a heavy shower. And Ahab rode and went to Jezreel.*

46 *Then the hand of the LORD was on Elijah, and he girded up his loins and outran Ahab to Jezreel.*

Let's Ask Some Questions

(based on **1 Kings 18**)

Think back to 1 Kings 17. Where did God send Elijah then? Where does God send him now?

Who is Obadiah? How had God used him to be a provider?

What is Obadiah's take on his boss and the boss's wife?

How does this help you understand why God told Elijah to hide in
1 Kings 17?

Briefly summarize the events that take place on Mount Carmel between
Elijah and the prophets of Baal.

How do you think you would have responded in the face of such an
enormous victory? How long do you think you'd have been encouraged?
Why?

What truths did you learn about *God* in this chapter?

Let's Read Again

Up to this point, God has sent Elijah to three different places. The first two times He sent him *away from* danger and *toward* provision. The third time, he sent him directly toward a showdown and then showed up to provide the big win!

Bottom line: God directed Elijah clearly and provided for him thoroughly even when he was in danger of literally starving and literally being killed at the hands of powerful (and crazy!) people. Keep that in mind as you read 1 Kings 19.

1 Kings 19

1 *Now Ahab told Jezebel all that Elijah had done, and how he had killed all the prophets with the sword.*

2 *Then Jezebel sent a messenger to Elijah, saying, "So may the gods do to me and even more, if I do not make your life as the life of one of them by tomorrow about this time."*

3 *And he was afraid and arose and ran for his life and came to Beersheba, which belongs to Judah, and left his servant there.*

4 *But he himself went a day's journey into the wilderness, and came and sat down under a juniper tree; and he requested for himself that he might die, and said, "It is enough; now, O LORD, take my life, for I am not better than my fathers."*

5 *He lay down and slept under a juniper tree; and behold, there was an angel touching him, and he said to him, "Arise, eat."*

6 *Then he looked and behold, there was at his head a bread cake baked on hot stones, and a jar of water. So he ate and drank and lay down again.*

7 *The angel of the LORD came again a second time and touched him and said, "Arise, eat, because the journey is too great for you."*

8　*So he arose and ate and drank, and went in the strength of that food forty days and forty nights to Horeb, the mountain of God.*

9　*Then he came there to a cave and lodged there; and behold, the word of the LORD came to him, and He said to him, "What are you doing here, Elijah?"*

10　*He said, "I have been very zealous for the LORD, the God of hosts; for the sons of Israel have forsaken Your covenant, torn down Your altars and killed Your prophets with the sword. And I alone am left; and they seek my life, to take it away."*

11　*So He said, "Go forth and stand on the mountain before the LORD." And behold, the LORD was passing by! And a great and strong wind was rending the mountains and breaking in pieces the rocks before the LORD; but the LORD was not in the wind. And after the wind an earthquake, but the LORD was not in the earthquake.*

12　*After the earthquake a fire, but the LORD was not in the fire; and after the fire a sound of a gentle blowing.*

13　*When Elijah heard it, he wrapped his face in his mantle and went out and stood in the entrance of the cave. And behold, a voice came to him and said, "What are you doing here, Elijah?"*

FYI:

Geography

Elijah runs from the mountain of his great victory—Mount Carmel in the northern kingdom of Israel—way down to the southernmost point of Judah in Beersheba . . . and then he keeps going further all the way down to Mount Horeb (also known as Mount Sinai), the mountain that we associate with Moses!

14　*Then he said, "I have been very zealous for the LORD, the God of hosts; for the sons of Israel have forsaken Your covenant, torn down Your altars and killed Your prophets with the sword. And I alone am left; and they seek my life, to take it away."*

15　*The LORD said to him, "Go, return on your way to the wilderness of Damascus, and when you have arrived, you shall anoint Hazael king over Aram;*

16　*and Jehu the son of Nimshi you shall anoint king over Israel; and Elisha the son of Shaphat of Abel-meholah you shall anoint as prophet in your place.*

17　*"It shall come about, the one who escapes from the sword of Hazael, Jehu shall put to death, and the one who escapes from the sword of Jehu, Elisha shall put to death.*

18　*"Yet I will leave 7,000 in Israel, all the knees that have not bowed to Baal and every mouth that has not kissed him."*

19　*So he departed from there and found Elisha the son of Shaphat, while he was plowing with twelve pairs of oxen before him, and he with the twelfth. And Elijah passed over to him and threw his mantle on him.*

20　*He left the oxen and ran after Elijah and said, "Please let me kiss my father and my mother, then I will follow you." And he said to him, "Go back again, for what have I done to you?"*

21　*So he returned from following him, and took the pair of oxen and sacrificed them and boiled their flesh with the implements of the oxen, and gave it to the people and they ate. Then he arose and followed Elijah and ministered to him.*

Let's Ask Some Questions

(based on **1 Kings 19**)

After standing against hundreds of false prophets and a nation of idolators, what ignites Elijah's fear?

How does Elijah react?

How does this compare with his actions in previous stressful or dangerous situations?

Think for a moment back to 1 Kings 17 and 18. When Elijah went places and did things in these chapters, what prompted him? What prompts him to move here in 1 Kings 19?

Let's Do Some Marking

Let's look a little more closely at what Elijah does when he gets out of Dodge! Underline:

> • Elijah's "actions"

1 Kings 19:3-8

3 And he was afraid and arose and ran for his life and came to
   Beersheba, which belongs to Judah, and left his servant there.

4 But he himself went a day's journey into the wilderness, and came
   and sat down under a juniper tree; and he requested for himself
   that he might die, and said, "It is enough; now, O LORD, take my
   life, for I am not better than my fathers."

5 He lay down and slept under a juniper tree; and behold, there was
   an angel touching him, and he said to him, "Arise, eat."

6 Then he looked and behold, there was at his head a bread cake
   baked on *hot stones, and a jar of water.* So he ate and drank and
   lay down again.

7 The angel of the LORD came again a second time and touched him
   and said, "Arise, eat, because the journey is too great for you."

8 So he arose and ate and drank, and went in the strength of that
   food forty days and forty nights to Horeb, the mountain of God.

Let's Ask Some More Questions

List what Elijah does in verses 3-8.

What does the angel of the LORD do for Elijah?

Can you relate? Have you ever been in a place of such spiritual weariness that all you wanted to do was go to sleep or check out entirely? If so, jot down the circumstances and as you do, realize the truth that *you are not alone!* If you are there now, jot it down knowing also that *there is hope!*

Up to this point, everything we've read has followed a pattern of God speaking and Elijah obeying. God says, "Go" and Elijah goes. We see something entirely different in 1 Kings 19. Instead of instructions, God leads with a question. Let's look more closely.

Let's Do Some Marking

Let's slow down and mark the following:

- God's repeated question to Elijah
- Elijah's repeated response to God

Remember to keep the full context in view as we look at these specific verses.

1 Kings 19:9-10, 13-14

9   *Then he came there to a cave and lodged there; and behold, the word of the LORD came to him, and He said to him, "What are you doing here, Elijah?"*

10   *He said, "I have been very zealous for the LORD, the God of hosts; for the sons of Israel have forsaken Your covenant, torn down Your altars and killed Your prophets with the sword. And I alone am left; and they seek my life, to take it away."*

13   *When Elijah heard it, he wrapped his face in his mantle and went out and stood in the entrance of the cave. And behold, a voice came to him and said, "What are you doing here, Elijah?"*

14   *Then he said, "I have been very zealous for the LORD, the God of hosts; for the sons of Israel have forsaken Your covenant, torn down Your altars and killed Your prophets with the sword. And I alone am left; and they seek my life, to take it away."*

Let's Ask Some More Questions

What is God's question to Elijah? How many times does He ask?

How does Elijah respond to God? What does he think about his own record, the people's record, and his situation?

What is true in Elijah's assessment? What is false? How do you know?

Can you relate? What are you telling yourself about your current situation? Are you telling yourself the truth?

If you are believing lies, what are they? What specific truth from God's Word can you hold up to them?

Obviously none of us today stands alone against idolatrous prophets and sociopathic monarchs. Still, we all know what it is to feel the weariness of "alone." Maybe you're the only Christian in your neighborhood and you've become weary of being the only salt and light on your block. Perhaps your school or workplace is filled with people who not only reject God, but are actively antagonistic.

Maybe you've found yourself in a hard ministry situation where everybody around you claims Jesus' name but lives like the world. Maybe you feel like a prisoner in your own home with little kids or other responsibilities that have you going day after day from morning until evening . . . without rest or help. The Bible says that the Church is the body of Christ, but you simply haven't seen it in action.

Weariness comes in a variety of packages and in many shapes and sizes. Sometimes it comes disguised. The good news is that our God didn't leave Elijah alone and He doesn't leave us alone either—even though we may *feel* alone at times! Let's finish with a few more questions from 1 Kings 19.

A Few More Questions

Although Elijah claimed that he alone was left, who does God direct him to in verse 16? What will this man do?

> 16 and Jehu the son of Nimshi you shall anoint king over Israel;
>   and Elisha the son of Shaphat of Abel-meholah you shall
>   anoint as prophet in your place.
>
> 17 "It shall come about, the one who escapes from the sword of
>   Hazael, Jehu shall put to death, and the one who escapes from
>   the sword of Jehu, Elisha shall put to death.
>
> 18 "Yet I will leave 7,000 in Israel, all the knees that have not
>   bowed to Baal and every mouth that has not kissed him."

What does this tell you about Elijah's perception of being the last prophet standing?

According to verse 18, how many other people are "with" Elijah? How many have not fallen to idolatry?

Before we call it a day, ask God to bring to your mind or cross your path with someone who will help you remember that you are not alone.

Let's Read

Finally, read Romans 8:28 and 35-39 to remind yourself about the love Christ has for you even when you feel persecuted and alone.

Romans 8:28, 35-39

28 *And we know that God causes all things to work together for good to those who love God, to those who are called according to His purpose.*

35 *Who will separate us from the love of Christ? Will tribulation, or distress, or persecution, or famine, or nakedness, or peril, or sword?*

36 *Just as it is written,*

"For Your sake we are being put to death all day long; We were considered as sheep to be slaughtered."

37 *But in all these things we overwhelmingly conquer through Him who loved us.*

38 *For I am convinced that neither death, nor life, nor angels, nor principalities, nor things present, nor things to come, nor powers,*

39 *nor height, nor depth, nor any other created thing, will be able to separate us from the love of God, which is in Christ Jesus our Lord.*

Just One Question

What difference does the love of God make? What does it do? How reliable is it?

EXTRA

Remember, this is bonus material to encourage and equip you, not to burden or weary you.

Leisure Reading or Listening

Keep up your leisure Bible reading! Share with someone else what you've been learning and applying from God's Word.

Intentional Encouragement

Reach out to someone this week and encourage that person in the Lord. Write down who you reached out to and how it was received.

Memorize Key Verses

Pick a key verse or two from 1 Kings 17–19, write it below, and commit it to memory.

#Hashtag It

Make a hashtag for 1 Kings 17–19.

"Post" It

Summarize what you've learned this week in 280 characters or less.

Now take 280 more characters to summarize how you're applying what you've learned!

Lesson Four

Sabbath: The Gift of Time

*"Then God blessed the seventh day and sanctified it,
because in it He rested from all His work which God had
created and made."*
—Genesis 2:3

In a world of 24 hours "on" for 7 days a week, the idea of Sabbath strikes us like a relic from a bygone era. The idea of delaying a purchase or activity because of a society-wide shutdown to rest seems inefficient and backwards in a world where we've become conditioned to grind our way forward on a treadmill that never sleeps.

Against the relentless pace of modern life stands the biblical concept of Sabbath, a set-apart day to stop, to worship, and to rest. Still practiced by Orthodox Jewish people worldwide, Sabbath no longer sets the rhythm for secular life in the Western world as it once did.

In fact, even in the church many Christians believe Sabbath belongs to the old covenant and see it now fulfilled in Christ, the One who brings true rest. Almost certainly you are bringing presuppositions to this lesson—whether you believe that Sabbath-keeping is relegated to the old covenant or whether you believe there is something in it for us today.

As we move into our lesson this week, let's acknowledge the bags we're carrying and see what God's Word itself says about Sabbath rest.

WHERE ARE YOU TODAY?

When you hear the word "Sabbath," what comes to mind?

Have you ever kept Sabbath by setting apart one day of the week to stop and to focus on God and rest? If so, why did you do this? What did it look like?

What is your current view about Sabbath (if you have one!)? Do you think Sabbath-keeping is required? Beneficial? Optional? Or something else? Explain.

Can you imagine how one set-apart day might impact your life? The life of your family?

SABBATH AT THE START

While we often think of Sabbath primarily as number four of the big ten given by God to the children of Israel at Mount Sinai, the concept shows up much earlier in the Bible than the giving of the Ten Commandments in Exodus 20. Sabbath precedes Moses and Abraham, even Noah and Abel.

God first introduces the concept of Sabbath rest on the seventh day of creation in the second chapter of Genesis. Sabbath, from the Hebrew root *shbt,* means to cease, to stop, or to rest.

We'll start with Genesis and work our way through some significant passages in early Exodus this week. Next week we'll make our way to Mount Sinai and eventually to Jesus as we explore what the Bible has to say about Sabbath rest.

Trace the Word through Scripture

In order to build a comprehensive view of a biblical topic, it's important to see what Scripture says throughout its pages. Often the first occurrence of a word can help us gain a strong foundation for the topic we're exploring.

LET'S EXPLORE!

The Bible opens with God speaking and creating! Genesis 1 records six days of activity where God creates light and brings the world as we know it into existence with waters and land, plants and animals. Day by day He creates and declares His creation good. At the end of six days He sees all that He has made, now including man, and declares it very good.

In describing the seventh day, the Hebrew root *shbt*—from which we get the word Sabbath—first appears in the text of Scripture twice translated as "rested." Let's take a look!

Let's Start by Marking

We'll begin by focusing our attention on God. Let's mark:

- references to *God*
- references to what God does

Then mark:

- references to *the seventh day*

Genesis 2:1-3

1 *Thus the heavens and the earth were completed, and all their hosts.*

2 *By the seventh day God completed His work which He had done, and He rested on the seventh day from all His work which He had done.*

3 *Then God blessed the seventh day and sanctified it, because in it He rested from all His work which God had created and made.*

A Few Questions

What does the text tell us about God? What specifically does it say that He has done?

Sabbath, Rest, Seventh

Sabbath and *rest* are both translated from the Hebrew root *shbt*.

We're also marking *seventh* because, while it is a different word, it is being used as a synonym.

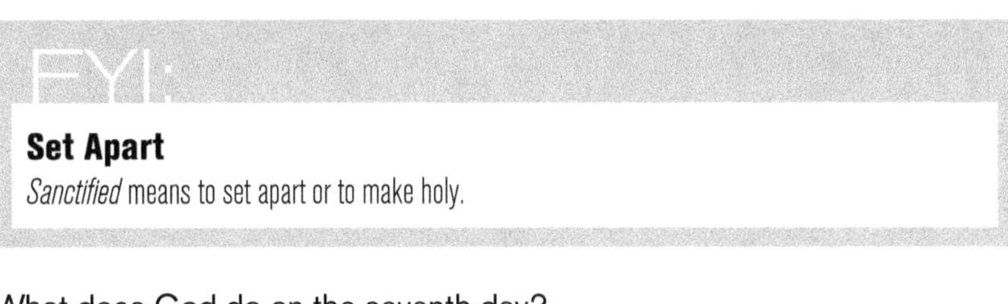

Set Apart

Sanctified means to set apart or to make holy.

What does God do on the seventh day?

How does God distinguish the seventh day from others?

Does God command anything about the Sabbath in this text? Think about your answer and respond with one sentence.

Just so we remember historical context, where are we with regard to salvation history? Are we before or after the fall?

The LORD Who Never Wearies

"Do you not know? Have you not heard? The Everlasting God, the LORD, the Creator of the ends of the earth does not become weary or tired. His understanding is inscrutable."

—Isaiah 40:28

How would you describe the state of the world and human beings when God rests on the seventh day?

Are there any questions about God and Sabbath that this text doesn't answer specifically? Make note of any that stood out to you and we'll see if any are answered as we continue to study!

Don't worry, we'll be applying soon! Let's explore some more texts before we dive in to that!

SABBATH AND THE PATRIARCHS

Although the concept of Sabbath bounds onto the biblical scene at the end of the creation account, there is no record of Sabbath as a rhythm of life for the generations from Adam to Noah or in the times of the patriarchs. We can't argue from silence that they didn't practice Sabbath, but we also cannot point to any recorded examples from their lives. Sabbath, after all, was modeled in creation but not commanded in the pre-fall world.

In the Genesis account, the One keeping Sabbath and likely pointing to a greater reality in the created order is God alone who works, completes His work, and rests.

THERE'S NO SABBATH IN EGYPT!

After creating His beautiful and good world, God rested. This was before sin, before the fall, before the brokenness of life as we know it today. Sabbath, while not commanded for humanity in the pre-fallen world, was part of God's original design. The One who never grows weary ceased on the seventh day.

By contrast, Exodus recounts life in Egypt where there was no rest for the Hebrews. Rest certainly would have been a welcome rhythm for those compelled by a tyrant to make brick after brick after brick, but Pharaoh would have none of it!

LET'S EXPLORE!

As we come to Exodus 5, Moses has his brother Aaron at his side and the support of his enslaved brethren who have believed the message that the LORD has seen their affliction and is about to act. It is after this encounter with the people that Moses goes to Pharaoh. The Hebrew root *shbt* is translated as "cease" in verse 5. Let's take a look!

Let's Mark

This time around, let's mark:

- any references to labor

Then, let's mark:

- *cease*

Exodus 5:1-9

1 *And afterward Moses and Aaron came and said to Pharaoh, "Thus says the LORD, the God of Israel, 'Let My people go that they may celebrate a feast to Me in the wilderness.' "*

2 *But Pharaoh said, "Who is the LORD that I should obey His voice to let Israel go? I do not know the LORD, and besides, I will not let Israel go."*

3   Then they said, "The God of the Hebrews has met with us. Please, let us go a three days' journey into the wilderness that we may sacrifice to the LORD our God, otherwise He will fall upon us with pestilence or with the sword."

4   But the king of Egypt said to them, "Moses and Aaron, why do you draw the people away from their work? Get back to your labors!"

5   Again Pharaoh said, "Look, the people of the land are now many, and you would have them cease from their labors!"

6   So the same day Pharaoh commanded the taskmasters over the people and their foremen, saying,

7   "You are no longer to give the people straw to make brick as previously; let them go and gather straw for themselves.

8   "But the quota of bricks which they were making previously, you shall impose on them; you are not to reduce any of it. Because they are lazy, therefore they cry out, 'Let us go and sacrifice to our God.'

9   "Let the labor be heavier on the men, and let them work at it so that they will pay no attention to false words."

A Few Questions . . .

What message does Moses bring from the LORD to Pharaoh?

How does Pharaoh respond? What is his initial objection?

How does Pharaoh specifically object in verses 4 and 5? How would the Hebrews going to worship God affect their labor?

How does the text describe the lives of the Hebrew slaves? Was the work ever over?

What action does Pharaoh take in response? What does this show about the people's position and his view of them?

Can you relate to work that never ceases, to quotas that keep increasing? In what ways?

How does working for Pharaoh compare with the work God modeled in the Garden of Eden?

THE GIFT OF SABBATH

While Sabbath-keeping is well-known to be the fourth of the Ten Commandments, the always-on Hebrew slaves first encounter the practice of Sabbath not just as a commandment but as a gift from God prior to Moses receiving the Law at Mount Sinai.

LET'S EXPLORE!

Exodus 14 tells of God's actions on behalf of Israel in delivering her from her Egyptian oppressors, and the beginning of Exodus 15 records Israel's song of praise in response. As we pick up in Exodus 16, God provides both manna and rest.

Let's Mark

In both excerpts from Exodus, let's mark:

- references to *sabbath*, *rest,* and *seventh day*
- references to the *sixth day*

Exodus 16:4-5

4 *Then the LORD said to Moses, "Behold, I will rain bread from heaven for you; and the people shall go out and gather a day's portion every day, that I may test them, whether or not they will walk in My instruction.*

5 *"On the sixth day, when they prepare what they bring in, it will be twice as much as they gather daily."*

Exodus 16:22-30

22 *Now on the sixth day they gathered twice as much bread, two omers for each one. When all the leaders of the congregation came and told Moses,*

23   then he said to them, "This is what the LORD meant: Tomorrow is a sabbath observance, a holy sabbath to the LORD. Bake what you will bake and boil what you will boil, and all that is left over put aside to be kept until morning."

24   So they put it aside until morning, as Moses had ordered, and it did not become foul nor was there any worm in it.

25   Moses said, "Eat it today, for today is a sabbath to the LORD; today you will not find it in the field.

26   "Six days you shall gather it, but on the seventh day, the sabbath, there will be none."

27   It came about on the seventh day that some of the people went out to gather, but they found none.

28   Then the LORD said to Moses, "How long do you refuse to keep My commandments and My instructions?

29   "See, the LORD has given you the sabbath; therefore He gives you bread for two days on the sixth day. Remain every man in his place; let no man go out of his place on the seventh day."

30   So the people rested on the seventh day.

A Few Questions . . .

How much manna were the children of Israel to gather daily?

How was this instruction different on the sixth and seventh days?

> 4 Then the LORD said to Moses, "Behold, I will rain bread from heaven for you; and the people shall go out and gather a day's portion every day, that I may test them, whether or not they will walk in My instruction.
>
> 29 "See, the LORD has given you the sabbath; therefore He gives you bread for two days on the sixth day. Remain every man in his place; let no man go out of his place on the seventh day."

EXODUS 16:4 AND 29

What did you learn from marking *sabbath*, *rest,* and *seventh day*?

How does verse 29 describe the sabbath? What are the implications?

How else did the daily manna function according to verse 4?

When are you most aware of your dependence on God to provide daily bread?

What was Israel's part in having food to eat on the seventh day?

How did manna life compare with Pharaoh life?

Final Questions for the Week . . .

We'll look at Sabbath in the context of the fourth commandment next week, and we'll see what Jesus has to say about it. In the meantime . . .

Does thinking of Sabbath in terms of design and gift change your view of it?

What has been your most significant discovery from our Scripture texts this week?

EXTRA

Remember, this is bonus material to encourage and equip you, not to burden or weary you.

Leisure Reading or Listening

Keep up your leisure reading in the Word! Share with someone else what you've been learning and applying from Scripture.

Intentional Encouragement

Reach out to someone this week and encourage that person in the Lord. Write down who you reached out to and how it was received.

Memorize Key Verses

Pick a key verse or two from this week's lesson, write it below, and commit it to memory.

#Hashtag It

Make a hashtag for what you learned about Sabbath this week.
(Remember, we have more to go next week!)

"Post" It

Summarize what you've learned this week in 280 characters or less.

Now take 280 more characters to summarize how you're applying what
you've learned!

Sabbath: Sinai and Beyond!

"For if Joshua had given them rest, He would not have spoken of another day after that. So there remains a Sabbath rest for the people of God."
—Hebrews 4:8-9

What was first displayed in the Garden of Eden and shown to be a gift in the wilderness becomes codified at Mount Sinai when Moses receives the tablets of the Law written by the finger of God. At Sinai, God commands His people to practice Sabbath and explains the scope and reason in surprising detail.

The Ten Commandments appear twice in the Torah, the first five books of the Bible. They're first recorded in Exodus 20 when the children of Israel are at Mount Sinai only about 3 months removed from Egypt. Moses recounts the words again when the people are poised at the edge of the promised land in Deuteronomy 5 nearly forty years later.

In each passage, nearly 30% of the Decalogue—from the Greek for "ten words"—is devoted to the Sabbath commands which extended not only to all people, but to their animals as well.

WHERE ARE YOU TODAY?

What was your biggest takeaway from studying about Sabbath last week?

What questions are you hoping to resolve this week?

SABBATH AS COMMAND AT SINAI

In Exodus 20, Moses records the Ten Commandments which were given to him by God on Mount Sinai about three months after their exodus from Egypt.

In Deuteronomy 5, Moses reminds the people of the Ten Commandments before they enter the promised land forty years later.

Let's Start by Marking

Let's mark:

- references to *sabbath*, *rest,* and *seventh day*
- references to *work* and *six*
- the word *remember*

LET'S EXPLORE!

In each of the passages, Moses teaches the people about the fourth commandment. As you read and mark, note the similarities and differences.

Exodus 20:8-11

8 *"Remember the sabbath day, to keep it holy.*

9 *"Six days you shall labor and do all your work,*

10 *but the seventh day is a sabbath of the LORD your God; in it you shall not do any work, you or your son or your daughter, your male or your female servant or your cattle or your sojourner who stays with you.*

11 *"For in six days the LORD made the heavens and the earth, the sea and all that is in them, and rested on the seventh day; therefore the LORD blessed the sabbath day and made it holy.*

Deuteronomy 5:13-15

13 *'Six days you shall labor and do all your work,*

14 *but the seventh day is a sabbath of the LORD your God; in it you shall not do any work, you or your son or your daughter or your male servant or your female servant or your ox or your donkey or any of your cattle or your sojourner who stays with you, so that your male servant and your female servant may rest as well as you.*

15 *'You shall remember that you were a slave in the land of Egypt, and the LORD your God brought you out of there by a mighty hand and by an outstretched arm; therefore the LORD your God commanded you to observe the sabbath day.*

A Few Questions . . .

According to Exodus 20:8, what were the people to do with regard to the Sabbath?

What were they to do on the other six days?

To whom does the Sabbath command apply?

What do you think is significant about the command's scope? Is there anything that surprises you? If so, what and why?

What biblical account grounds the commandment in the Exodus account?

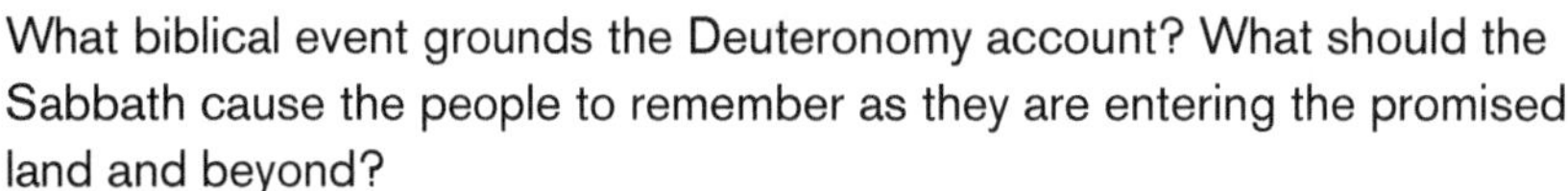

What biblical event grounds the Deuteronomy account? What should the Sabbath cause the people to remember as they are entering the promised land and beyond?

How is your work/rest balance? Do you take a Sabbath day? Does your life reflect God's design, or do you think it reveals a bondage of some sort? Explain.

How does your work/rest balance (or imbalance) affect those in your circle of influence? Family? Friends? Co-workers? Employees?

Do you more often need a reminder to work or to rest? Why do you think this is? If you're imbalanced, what corrective truth do you need to remember?

If a culture followed this pattern, how do you think it would affect always-on salaried workers? Overworked hourly employees? How would it affect the way that culture looks at and treats other people?

Digging Deeper

The Example of Nehemiah

If you have some extra time this week, take an hour or so to read through the Old Testament book of Nehemiah. Nehemiah lived in exile in Susa and served as a cupbearer to the king before God sent him on the adventure of a lifetime to return to the land of Judah to rebuild the wall of Jerusalem.

As you read, note what you can learn from Nehemiah about when to stop and when to refuse to stop. Record what you discover below.

SABBATH AS SIGN, COVENANT, REMINDER

In Exodus 31, God speaks again to Moses regarding the Sabbath after giving him instructions on how to build and furnish the tabernacle.

The children of Israel had a great work ahead of them in constructing this holy structure, but that was not to stop their rhythm of rest.

Let's Start by Marking

Let's mark:

- references to *sabbath*, *rest*, and *seventh day*
- references to *six*
- references to *the LORD*

LET'S EXPLORE!

Moses receives these words on Mount Sinai while the people below are building a golden calf.

Exodus 31:12-18

12 *The LORD spoke to Moses, saying,*

13 *"But as for you, speak to the sons of Israel, saying, 'You shall surely observe My sabbaths; for this is a sign between Me and you throughout your generations, that you may know that I am the LORD who sanctifies you.*

14 *'Therefore you are to observe the sabbath, for it is holy to you. Everyone who profanes it shall surely be put to death; for whoever does any work on it, that person shall be cut off from among his people.*

15 *'For six days work may be done, but on the seventh day there is a sabbath of complete rest, holy to the LORD; whoever does any work on the sabbath day shall surely be put to death.*

16 *'So the sons of Israel shall observe the sabbath, to celebrate the sabbath throughout their generations as a perpetual covenant.'*

17 *"It is a sign between Me and the sons of Israel forever; for in six days the LORD made heaven and earth, but on the seventh day He ceased from labor, and was refreshed."*

18 *When He had finished speaking with him upon Mount Sinai, He gave Moses the two tablets of the testimony, tablets of stone, written by the finger of God.*

A Few Questions . . .

Who is Moses speaking to in these verses? Whose message is he bringing?

How is the Sabbath described in verse 13? What is its function and duration?

What are the people called to do . . . and not do on the Sabbath?

What will it cause Israel to know about the Lord, according to verse 13?

How can this serve as a corrective for people who think they can somehow make themselves right in God's eyes?

Punishable by Death

While we have a hard time wrapping our minds around not keeping Sabbath as a capital offense (Exodus 35:2), we don't live in a theocratic government bound in covenant to God. It's easy for us to trivialize the situation and think, "It's pretty harsh to be put to death for not taking a nap," but that wasn't what was happening. Because Sabbath was a sign of the covenant at Sinai, not keeping Sabbath was essentially breaking a solemn binding agreement with God—and that is serious business.

What consequences are tied with profaning the Sabbath in this passage?

How else is the Sabbath described in verse 16? How can this help us understand the harsh consequences associated with profaning it?

What verb is attached to the Sabbath in verses 13, 14, and 16? What other verb do we see in verse 16? How do these relate?

What is the Sabbath grounded in according to verse 17?

What do we learn about the Lord throughout this passage?

What does Sabbath accomplish according to this passage?

THE LORD OF THE SABBATH HEALS

No one but Jesus ever fully kept the Law, and yet the Jewish leaders regularly accused Him of breaking it, particularly with regard to the Sabbath. Their version of the law, however, was a bulked up, over-defined, man-made code that added on to the true Law given by God. Jesus displayed in His life and teaching the truth about Sabbath.

Let's Start by Marking

Let's keep marking:

- references to *Sabbath*

LET'S EXPLORE!

This account of Jesus and His hungry disciples appears in all three of the synoptic gospels.

Mark 2:23-28 (see also Matthew 12:1-14, Luke 6:1-11)

23 *And it happened that He was passing through the grainfields on the Sabbath, and His disciples began to make their way along while picking the heads of grain.*

24 *The Pharisees were saying to Him, "Look, why are they doing what is not lawful on the Sabbath?"*

25 *And He said to them, "Have you never read what David did when he was in need and he and his companions became hungry;*

26 *how he entered the house of God in the time of Abiathar the high priest, and ate the consecrated bread, which is not lawful for anyone to eat except the priests, and he also gave it to those who were with him?"*

27 Jesus said to them, "The Sabbath was made for man, and not man

for the Sabbath.

28 "So the Son of Man is Lord even of the Sabbath."

A Few Questions . . .

What are Jesus' disciples doing that stirs up the Pharisees?

What accusation do the Pharisees make in verse 24?

How does Jesus respond? What biblical precedent does He cite?

What two greater principles does He follow up with in verses 27 and 28?

Based on what you've seen so far in Scripture, in what way does
Scripture show that the Sabbath was made for man?

How have you seen this to be true in your life?

What implication does Jesus' statement that He is Lord of the Sabbath have?

FREEDOM FROM BONDAGE . . . AGAIN!

As we come to this next Jesus and Sabbath passage, let's keep in mind the words of Deuteronomy 5:15.

Let's Start by Marking

Let's mark:

- references to *freedom, releasing* and *untying*
- references to *bondage* and *bond*

LET'S EXPLORE!

This particular non-emergent Sabbath healing is only recorded by Dr. Luke.

Luke 13:10-17

10　*And He was teaching in one of the synagogues on the Sabbath.*

11　*And there was a woman who for eighteen years had had a sickness caused by a spirit; and she was bent double, and could not straighten up at all.*

12　*When Jesus saw her, He called her over and said to her, "Woman, you are freed from your sickness."*

13　*And He laid His hands on her; and immediately she was made erect again and* began *glorifying God.*

> **Deuteronomy 5:15**
> "You shall remember that you were a slave in the land of Egypt, and the LORD your God brought you out of there by a mighty hand and by an outstretched arm; therefore the LORD your God commanded you to observe the sabbath day."

14 *But the synagogue official, indignant because Jesus had healed on the Sabbath,* began *saying to the crowd in response, "There are six days in which work should be done; so come during them and get healed, and not on the Sabbath day."*

15 *But the Lord answered him and said, "You hypocrites, does not each of you on the Sabbath untie his ox or his donkey from the stall and lead him away to water* him?

16 *"And this woman, a daughter of Abraham as she is, whom Satan has bound for eighteen long years, should she not have been released from this bond on the Sabbath day?"*

17 *As He said this, all His opponents were being humiliated; and the entire crowd was rejoicing over all the glorious things being done by Him.*

A Few Questions . . .

Who meets Jesus in this passage and on what day of the week?

What is her situation? How long has she been in this condition and why?

What does Jesus say to her in verse 12? Where else did you note the contrast between freedom and bondage words in this passage?

Think back to Deuteronomy 5:15. What was one truth that the Israelites were to remember on Sabbath?

What issue does the synagogue official have with Jesus? What commandment does He accuse Jesus of breaking?

How does Jesus respond? How does He ground His action in a correct interpretation and application of the fourth commandment?

This may go without saying, but who freed the Hebrews from Pharaoh? Who is freeing this woman on the Sabbath?

Digging Deeper

Sabbath Fails

If you have time this week, you may want to investigate one or more of the Sabbath Fail chapters. Each of the major prophets addresses Sabbath failure and its consequences on God's people. If you're thinking "What about Daniel?" remember that his entire life takes place in Babylonian captivity while the land enjoys its Sabbath rest (see 2 Chronicles 36:20-21).

As you explore these chapters, ask:

• What have the people done . . . or not done?

• What consequence has come?

• What remedy remains?

Isaiah 58

Jeremiah 17

Ezekiel 20

A SABBATH REMAINS

While Jesus both kept the true Sabbath and fulfilled it, the author of Hebrews tells his readers that there is also a Sabbath that remains yet future for the people of God. Let's take a look at two final passages.

Let's Start by Marking

Let's mark:

- *Sabbath*
- and *shadow*

LET'S EXPLORE!

When is this reiterated?

Colossians 2:16

16 *Therefore no one is to act as your judge in regard to food or drink or in respect to a festival or a new moon or a Sabbath day—*

17 *things which are a mere shadow of what is to come; but the substance belongs to Christ.*

A Few Questions . . .

What is Sabbath grouped with in verse 16?

What are these things said to be in comparison to Christ?

Does Paul give any direction here as to whether someone should or should not set apart a day of rest? Explain.

What instruction does he give? What can we learn from this?

LET'S EXPLORE!

Since this is a little beyond the scope of our study, I will leave this here simply for you to read. The author of Hebrews reminds his (or her!) readers that there remains a Sabbath rest for the people of God. Rest in the Garden was perfect . . . and there remains a perfect eschatological rest.

When we set aside a day as the Jewish people were commanded, we remember God as Creator and Redeemer. We acknowledge the order of creation and we also remember that He is the One who set us free. As He set Israel free from Egypt, so also has He set believers free from the power of sin and death.

From Hebrews 4, we remember that we have true rest in Christ that is both now and not yet.

Hebrews 4

1 *Therefore, let us fear if, while a promise remains of entering His rest, any one of you may seem to have come short of it.*

2 *For indeed we have had good news preached to us, just as they also; but the word they heard did not profit them, because it was not united by faith in those who heard.*

3 *For we who have believed enter that rest, just as He has said,*

"As I swore in My wrath, They shall not enter My rest,"

although His works were finished from the foundation of the world.

4   For He has said somewhere concerning the seventh day: *"And God rested on the seventh day from all His works";*

5   and again in this passage, *"They shall not enter My rest."*

6   Therefore, since it remains for some to enter it, and those who formerly had good news preached to them failed to enter because of disobedience,

7   He again fixes a certain day,

"Today," saying through David after so long a time just as has been said before, "Today if you hear His voice, Do not harden your hearts."

8   For if Joshua had given them rest, He would not have spoken of another day after that.

9   So there remains a Sabbath rest for the people of God.

10   For the one who has entered His rest has himself also rested from his works, as God did from His.

11   Therefore let us be diligent to enter that rest, so that no one will fall, through following the same example of disobedience.

12   For the word of God is living and active and sharper than any two-edged sword, and piercing as far as the division of soul and spirit, of both joints and marrow, and able to judge the thoughts and intentions of the heart.

13   And there is no creature hidden from His sight, but all things are open and laid bare to the eyes of Him with whom we have to do.

14   Therefore, since we have a great high priest who has passed through the heavens, Jesus the Son of God, let us hold fast our confession.

15 *For we do not have a high priest who cannot sympathize with our*

  weaknesses, but One who has been tempted in all things as we are,

  yet *without sin.*

16 *Therefore let us draw near with confidence to the throne of grace,*

  so that we may receive mercy and find grace to help in time of

  need.

Final Questions for the Week . . .

What conclusions have you drawn on God's Sabbath after studying for
yourself?

What do you plan to do with what you've learned?

Take some time to ask God to help you obey in whatever way He is calling
you to respond to His Word.

EXTRA

Remember, this is bonus material to encourage and equip you, not to burden or weary you.

Leisure Reading or Listening

Keep up your leisure reading of God's Word! Share with someone else what you've been learning and applying.

Intentional Encouragement

Reach out to someone this week and encourage that person in the Lord. Write down who you reached out to and how it was received.

Memorize Key Verses

Pick a key verse or two from this week's lesson, write it below, and commit it to memory.

#Hashtag It

Make a hashtag for what you learned about Sabbath this week. (Or summarize your overall take from both weeks!)

"Post" It

Summarize what you've learned this week in 280 characters or less.

Now take 280 more characters to summarize how you're applying what you've learned!

Guard Your Mind

> *"And the peace of God, which surpasses all comprehension, will guard your hearts and your minds in Christ Jesus."*
> —Philippians 4:7

Weariness often starts in the heart and mind when we allow deception to unseat the truth of God's Word. Full-on lies and even (maybe especially!) little half-truths have a way of eroding our view of God and His truth, thereby weakening us for the fight. It often starts small as we ruminate on thoughts like, "No good deed goes unpunished, does it?" and before we know it, the lie has breached the wall.

As believers, we do not battle merely against flesh and blood, Paul reminds us of this clearly in Ephesians 6. "Our struggle is not against flesh and blood, but against the rulers, against the powers, against the world forces of this darkness, against the spiritual *forces* of wickedness in the heavenly *places*" (Ephesians 6:12). Because of this we are to resist and stand firm, wearing God's armor.

Jesus talks about our enemy in several unsavory ways. He is a thief who sets out to steal, kill, and destroy (John 10:10). He is like a lion seeking someone to swallow up (1 Peter 5:8). He is also the father of lies—lying being his very nature (John 8:44).

If our enemy traffics in lies, it is imperative that we learn to guard our minds and stand firm in truth.

WHERE ARE YOU TODAY?

As we get started this week, take some time to prayerfully think through where we've been on this journey.

Have you taken the opportunity to incorporate some Sabbaths into your life? If so, how is it going?

Are you beginning to win the battle over weariness? Explain.

GUARD YOUR MIND

In his letter to the church at Philippi, Paul writes arguably his most encouraging and uplifting letter from—of all places—a Roman prison. While the letter teems with joy, context clearly reveals that the church of Philippi struggled with some unity problems.

Let's Start by Marking

Let's mark:

- references to *the peace of God*
- all-or-nothing words
- actions Paul's readers are to take . . . or not take
- references to *the Lord*

LET'S EXPLORE!

In an actionable concluding chapter to his letter to the Philippians, Paul instructs his readers on how to steward their minds.

Philippians 4:4-9

4 *Rejoice in the Lord always; again I will say, rejoice!*

5 *Let your gentle* spirit *be known to all men. The Lord is near.*

6 *Be anxious for nothing, but in everything by prayer and supplication with thanksgiving let your requests be made known to God.*

7 *And the peace of God, which surpasses all comprehension, will guard your hearts and your minds in Christ Jesus.*

8 *Finally, brethren, whatever is true, whatever is honorable, whatever is right, whatever is pure, whatever is lovely, whatever is of good repute, if there is any excellence and if anything worthy of praise, dwell on these things.*

9 *The things you have learned and received and heard and seen in me, practice these things, and the God of peace will be with you.*

A Few Questions . . .

What does Paul tell the Philippians to do in verses 4-6?

What does he tell them *not* to do in the same verses?

> ## PHILIPPIANS 4:4-7
>
> 4 *Rejoice in the Lord always; again I will say, rejoice!*
>
> 5 *Let your gentle spirit be known to all men. The Lord is near.*
>
> 6 *Be anxious for nothing, but in everything by prayer and supplication with thanksgiving let your requests be made known to God.*
>
> 7 *And the peace of God, which surpasses all comprehension, will guard your hearts and your minds in Christ Jesus.*

What does Paul write about the Lord in these verses?

How does what Paul says about God impact what he has told them to do?

How would you summarize the impact of God's presence on situations that often cause anxiety?

Considering verse 7, what does Paul say will result from submitting to the truth?

Is there a particular situation today where you need the peace of God?

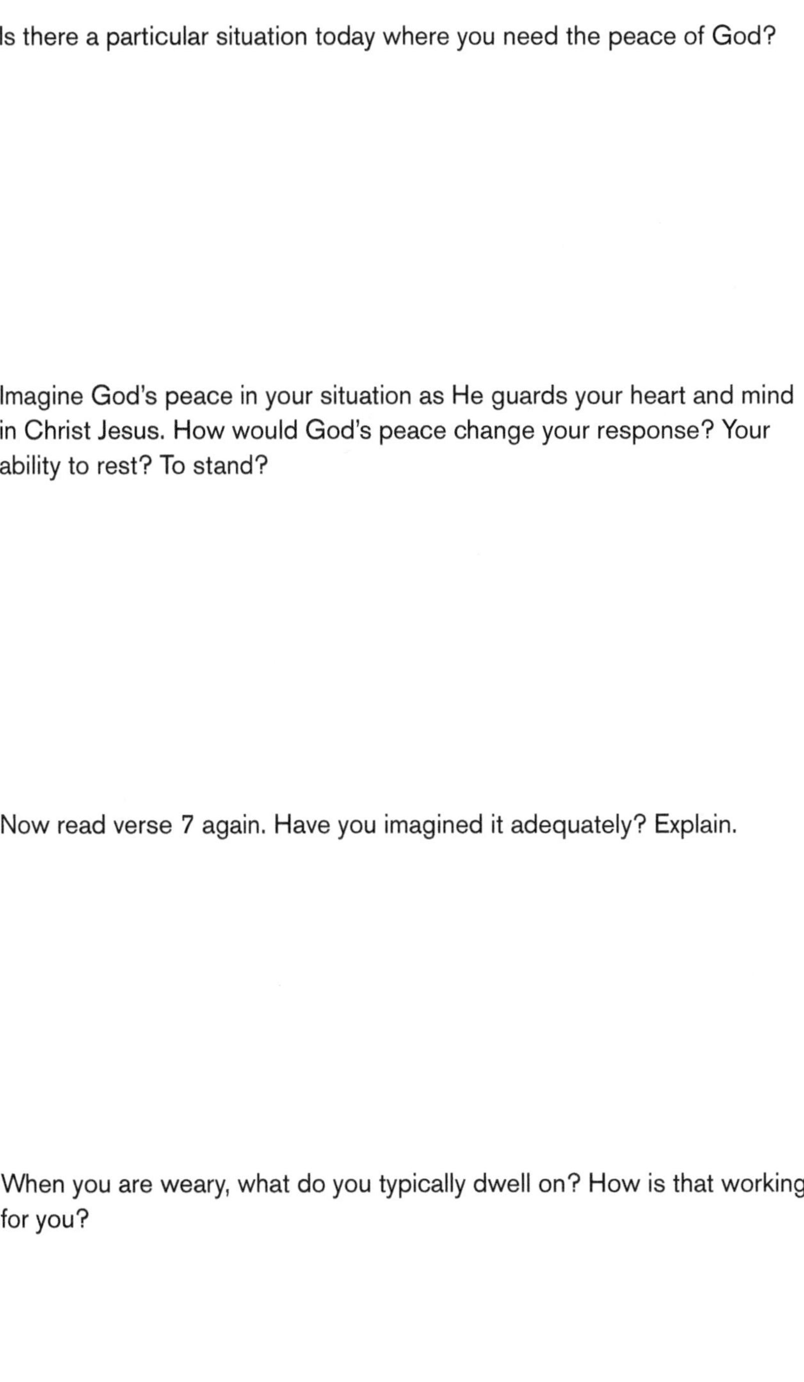

Imagine God's peace in your situation as He guards your heart and mind in Christ Jesus. How would God's peace change your response? Your ability to rest? To stand?

Now read verse 7 again. Have you imagined it adequately? Explain.

When you are weary, what do you typically dwell on? How is that working for you?

> 8 *Finally, brethren, whatever is true, whatever is honorable, whatever is right, whatever is pure, whatever is lovely, whatever is of good repute, if there is any excellence and if anything worthy of praise, dwell on these things.*
>
> 9 *The things you have learned and received and heard and seen in me, practice these things, and the God of peace will be with you.*

PHILIPPIANS 4:8-9

What does Paul tell the Philippians to dwell on?

If there is something today that has you weary, write it down and run it through the Philippians 4:8 rubric: Is it true? Is it honorable? And so forth. Use all the space you need!

How does Paul close this section in verse 9?

Are there examples you have followed (or follow) that lead you away from peace? Explain.

How can you correct that and begin to follow God's way instead?

TAKING THOUGHTS CAPTIVE

Paul regularly writes about the importance of right thinking—having our minds renewed (Romans 12:2, Ephesians 4:23) so that instead of operating with worldly wisdom, we set our minds on things above (Colossians 3:2, 1 Corinthians 2:16).

In 2 Corinthians 10 he uses combat language when he talks about taking thoughts captive to the obedience of Christ. While the context points to his interactions with those who don't yet know Jesus and, thus, focuses on evangelism, there is grounded application in these verses for us today.

Let's Start by Marking

Let's mark:

- references to *flesh*
- references to *destruction* and *destroying*; *weapons, war,* and *warfare*
- references to *God* and *Christ*

LET'S EXPLORE!

As we come to the passage, Paul describes himself and his Gospel work. In verses 1-2 he has just said that he is meek face-to-face, but bold when absent.

2 Corinthians 10:3-6

3 For though we walk in the flesh, we do not war according to the flesh,

4 for the weapons of our warfare are not of the flesh, but divinely powerful for the destruction of fortresses.

5 We are destroying speculations and every lofty thing raised up against the knowledge of God, and we are taking every thought captive to the obedience of Christ,

6 and we are ready to punish all disobedience, whenever your obedience is complete.

A Few Questions . . .

How does Paul describe the work that he and his associates are doing?

Digging Deeper

Thinking Throughout Scripture

What do different parts of Scripture teach us about guarding our thinking and/or renewing our minds?

OLD TESTAMENT
Torah

History

Prophets

Wisdom Literature

NEW TESTAMENT
Gospels

Acts

Paul's Letters

General Epistles

Prophecy

2 CORINTHIANS 10:4-5

> 4 for the weapons of our warfare are not of the flesh, but
>   divinely powerful for the destruction of fortresses.
>
> 5 We are destroying speculations and every lofty thing raised
>   up against the knowledge of God, and we are taking every
>   thought captive to the obedience of Christ,

What are they destroying? How are they described in verses 4 and 5?

What are some current examples of ideologies or thoughts that are raised up against the knowledge of God?

What is the standard of truth according to Paul? What outcome is he pursuing at the end of verse 5?

Again, while verse 6 in particular shows that Paul and his associates were engaged in changing the minds of unbelievers, what implication does this have for our thinking?

Where does your mind go if left "unattended"? Where does it default?

Are you aware when your mind is acting up on you? When you've allowed it to stray from truth? If so, what symptoms do you notice?

Do you think this ever contributes to weariness? If so, how and to what extent?

Does your mind ever race with speculations that come up against the knowledge of God? Where does it go? If so, what does Paul tell us to do?

How can you use truth to take your thoughts captive to the obedience of Christ?

A SONG OF ASCENT

The Songs of Ascent were likely sung by Jewish people while traveling uphill to Jerusalem to celebrate the three major annual feasts. This particular psalm is attributed to David's son, King Solomon.

Let's Start by Marking

Let's mark:

- references to *vain*
- references to human effort
- references to *the Lord*

LET'S EXPLORE!

Although this psalm is 6 verses long, we'll focus only on the first two verses.

Psalm 127:1-2

A Song of Ascents, of Solomon.

1   *Unless the LORD builds the house,*

    They labor in vain who build it;

    Unless the LORD guards the city,

    The watchman keeps awake in vain.

2   *It is vain for you to rise up early,*

    To retire late,

    To eat the bread of painful labors;

    For He gives to His beloved even in his sleep.

A Few Questions . . .

Let's consider what Solomon says about house building in verse 1.

What does a built house assume? What does it require of man?

What tension do you see in the text? What else does Solomon say it requires?

What does it mean to labor in vain?

Have you ever found yourself laboring in vain? If so, what happened? How did you know?

Vain

The Hebrew word used here, *shav,* means emptiness or nothingness. To labor in vain, then, is to labor to no end, for no purpose.

> **PSALM 127:1B-2**
>
> 1B *Unless the Lord guards the city,*
>   *The watchman keeps awake in vain.*
>
> 2   *It is vain for you to rise up early,*
>   *To retire late,*
>   *To eat the bread of painful labors;*
>   *For He gives to His beloved even in his sleep.*

What similar argument does Solomon make in the second half of verse 1?

What will happen to the city if it is only guarded by a watchman?

What conclusion does Solomon come to in the second half of verse 2?

What in the text is parallel to "rising early" and "retiring late"?

Do you ever burn the candle at both ends, so to speak? If so, why and when?

How has that worked for you?

How can you practically apply Psalm 127 in your life this week?

Final Questions for the Week . . .

What practical steps can you take this week to guard your thinking?

What has been your biggest takeaway from our texts this week?

What do you plan to do with what you've learned?

EXTRA

Remember, this is bonus material to encourage and equip you, not to burden or weary you.

Leisure Reading or Listening

Keep up your leisure Bible reading! Share with someone else what you've been learning and applying.

Intentional Encouragement

Reach out to someone this week and encourage that person in the Lord. Write down who you reached out to and how it was received.

Memorize Key Verses

Pick a key verse or two from this week's lesson, write it below, and commit it to memory.

#Hashtag It

Make a hashtag for what you learned this week about guarding your mind.

"Post" It

Summarize what you've learned this week in 280 characters or less.

Now take 280 more characters to summarize how you're applying what you've learned!

Strengthening Yourself in the Lord

"Yet those who wait for the LORD
Will gain new strength;
They will mount up with *wings like eagles,*
They will run and not get tired,
They will walk and not become weary."
—Isaiah 40:31

We sing it, we quote it. We print it on mugs and t-shirts. "Those who wait upon the Lord will renew their strength . . . they will mount up with wings as eagles . . . they will run and not grow weary, they will walk and not faint . . . ." We know it; most of us from memory. So why are we still so weary? Why are we sludging along instead of soaring?

Maybe it has something to do with understanding the biblical word for "wait." Perhaps our problem rests in our knowledge of the One we're told to wait on! This week we'll focus on Isaiah 40:31, but in order to do that we're going to need to unpack it in context!

WHERE ARE YOU TODAY?

When you hear the phrase "wait on the Lord," what comes to mind?

Have you ever experienced God's strength in a rise-up-with-wings-like-eagles fashion? If so, what were the circumstances?

What truths have you been applying from what we've learned so far in our study together?

Are you seeing any difference in your attitude and actions? If so, how?

Have you been aware of others in your life God has supplied to you so that you can know that you are not alone? Explain.

Isaiah 38 and 39

If you have time this week, you'll find it helpful to read Isaiah 38 and 39 for additional context. They tell about a good king who could have ended better.

WAITING ON THE LORD

Waiting rarely sits well with human beings. Whether we're queued up at Disney World or anticipating results from a medical test, waiting makes us aware of our lack of control over our time and circumstances. On a fundamental level, it makes us aware that "There is a God and I am not Him."

In God's economy, however, waiting on Him offers unimaginable promise. While we'll explore all of Isaiah 40 together, let's start with the power-packed final verse.

Let's Start by Marking

Let's mark:

- references to the people who wait for the LORD (including the pronouns)
- the benefits these people experience

Isaiah 40:31

31 Yet those who wait for the LORD

Will gain new strength;

They will mount up with wings like eagles,

They will run and not get tired,

They will walk and not become weary.

Let's Ask Some Questions

What are the positive benefits that will come to those who "wait for the LORD"? What negatives will they avoid?

A GLIMPSE INTO A PROMISED FUTURE

When we come to know the faithfulness of God, actively waiting on Him and hoping in Him brings strength. All of Isaiah 40 lays the foundation of the power and goodness of God, building the case that He can be trusted and that actively hoping in His provision will provide the strength we need.

Before we jump in, though, we need a bit of backstory. (Let's see if I can do this in one paragraph!) Way back in Genesis, God promised Abraham that He would make him into a great nation. Abraham had a son named Isaac. Isaac had twins: Jacob and Esau. God would change Jacob's name to Israel and fulfill the promise to Abraham through his line. (Esau's people would become the Edomites.) The people of Israel end up in Egypt during a time of great famine. While there they are eventually enslaved and grow from a clan into a nation. After 430 years in Egypt, God delivers them from Pharaoh by the hand of Moses in an event we refer to as the Exodus.

After the deaths of Moses and of Joshua, who succeeds him, the Israelites are ruled first by judges, then by kings. By the time of Isaiah 39, the once united nation of 12 tribes has been divided into two separate kingdoms. The northern kingdom of Israel has already been conquered by the Assyrians (in 722 BC) and the impending captivity of the southern kingdom of Judah and the destruction of the temple in Jerusalem (coming in 586 BC) have been prophesied. (Okay, I took two paragraphs! ;)

Long story short: Between the end of Isaiah 39 (where Isaiah recounts the end of King Hezekiah's life and prophesies the Babylonian captivity) and the beginning of Isaiah 40, about 150 years pass. Isaiah looks forward to the day when the prophecy has come true and addresses a future captivity-weary people.

FYI:

What does it mean to "wait"?

Translated from the Hebrew *qawah*, "wait" is not a passive "Oh well!" behavior. Waiting on God involves looking for, hoping in, and flat-out expecting God to deliver . . . then living in the reality of that life-strengthening truth!

LET'S READ

Take some time to read Isaiah 40 in your Bible or listen to it. We'll look at portions of it more closely and ask questions as we go.

LET'S EXPLORE!

Don't worry, we'll be marking later in this chapter. For now, just answer the questions to put us in context.

Isaiah 40:1-2

1 *"Comfort, O comfort My people," says your God.*

2 *"Speak kindly to Jerusalem;*

   And call out to her, that her warfare has ended,

   That her iniquity has been removed,

   That she has received of the LORD's hand

   Double for all her sins."

Let's Ask Some Questions

How does God tell the prophet to speak to this captivity-weary people? What specifically does He tell him to do? How does He tell him to do it?

What message does God send?

Considering the events of your life, are there ways that you relate to the people of Judah? If so, how?

There's no wonder the people of Judah were weary. Because of their iniquity, war had come to the country and many of the people had been taken into captivity in Babylon. God brought judgment on the people, but His anger would not endure forever. He sends His prophet to bring a good word to His weary people, a word kindly spoken to comfort them.

This God who comforted Judah is referred to in the New Testament book of 2 Corinthians as "the God of all comfort who comforts us in all our afflictions" (1:3-4). If you're weary today, remember that your God is the God of all comfort . . . and one of the primary ways He comforts us today is through His Word, because through it we come to know Him more and more!

LET'S EXPLORE!

Let's continue exploring our context and answer some simple questions from the text.

Isaiah 40:3-5

3 A voice is calling,

   "Clear the way for the LORD in the wilderness;

   Make smooth in the desert a highway for our God.

4 "Let every valley be lifted up,

   And every mountain and hill be made low;

   And let the rough ground become a plain,

   And the rugged terrain a broad valley;

5 Then the glory of the LORD will be revealed,

   And all flesh will see it together;

   For the mouth of the LORD has spoken."

Let's Ask Some More Questions

What is the voice calling out in these verses?

How would these words have provided hope for a captive people?

What hope can they give you today?

LET'S EXPLORE!

Get your pencils ready; we'll be marking in the next section.

Isaiah 40:6-8

6 *A voice says, "Call out."*

   Then he answered, "What shall I call out?"

   All flesh is grass, and all its loveliness is like the flower of the field.

7 *The grass withers, the flower fades,*

   When the breath of the LORD blows upon it;

   Surely the people are grass.

8 *The grass withers, the flower fades,*

   But the word of our God stands forever.

The Voice

Before there was *The Voice* on television, there was The Voice in Isaiah! If you have some extra time this week, read John 1:19-23 and Mark 1:1-3 to see how this relates to the New Testament and the coming of Jesus!

Let's Ask Some More Questions

How does the voice in verse 6 differ from the previous voice? Whose voice do you think this is and why?

What is the message called out in verses 6-8?

What characteristic separates God's Word from everything that it's compared to?

Keep this in mind as we look at the following verses about God and words that will stand forever!

Let's Mark

As we look at the remainder of Isaiah 40, let's focus our attention on our God *on* Whom we are to wait and *in* Whom we are to hope.

Let's mark:

- references to God (including pronouns)
- any associated truths you learn about Him (what He does or is)

As we go, I'll interject questions, but throughout the rest of Isaiah 40, let's keep marking references to God and any associated truths about Him. Just an aside here—marking references to new things you learn about God is always a good plan whenever you're reading Scripture!

Isaiah 40:9-31

9 *Get yourself up on a high mountain,*

   O Zion, bearer of good news,

   Lift up your voice mightily,

   O Jerusalem, bearer of good news;

   Lift it up, do not fear.

   Say to the cities of Judah,

   "Here is your God!"

10 *Behold, the Lord GOD will come with might,*

   With His arm ruling for Him.

   Behold, His reward is with Him

   And His recompense before Him.

11 *Like a shepherd He will tend His flock,*

   In His arm He will gather the lambs

   And carry them in His bosom;

   He will gently lead the nursing ewes.

A Few Questions

According to these verses, why doesn't Judah need to fear?

What does God do?

What is He likened to?

Think for a moment about your weariness. Could you give it in to the hands of a mighty warrior? What about a tender shepherd? Which do you need more in your life right now and why?

If this isn't enough, the prophet goes on . . .

12 *Who has measured the waters in the hollow of His hand,*

And marked off the heavens by the span,

And calculated the dust of the earth by the measure,

And weighed the mountains in a balance

And the hills in a pair of scales?

13 *Who has directed the Spirit of the LORD,*

Or as His counselor has informed Him?

14 With whom did He consult and who gave Him understanding?

And who taught Him in the path of justice and taught Him knowledge

And informed Him of the way of understanding?

A Few More Questions . . .

What is God like in comparison with the earth?

Does this help you in understanding His magnificence? If so, how?

What is God like in understanding?

What questions or problems do you need help in figuring out? Do you need justice somewhere in your life? Is this the kind of God you can trust? Explain.

FYI:

Romans 1:20—Creation Declares God

"For since the creation of the world His invisible attributes, His eternal power and divine nature, have been clearly seen, being understood through what has been made, so that they are without excuse."

Digging Deeper

Where Jesus Turned

While we will never bear the weight that Jesus did, we can learn from how
He faced it. If you have some extra time this week, read and consider Luke
22:39-46 as Jesus spends time in the Garden of Gethsemane on His way to the
cross to bear the sins of the world. (Matthew 26:36-46 and Mark 14:32-42 are
parallel accounts.)

What did Jesus do in the Garden?

What does Luke tell us about His condition?

What were the disciples doing and why?

There is more . . .

15 *Behold, the nations are like a drop from a bucket,*

   And are regarded as a speck of dust on the scales;

   Behold, He lifts up the islands like fine dust.

16 *Even Lebanon is not enough to burn,*

   Nor its beasts enough for a burnt offering.

17 *All the nations are as nothing before Him,*

   They are regarded by Him as less than nothing and meaningless.

A Few Questions

Do you have concerns about the world situation? About politics? About the Middle East? How does God compare to the nations?

What concerns do you have about vaccines, healthcare and its associated costs, pandemics, and the rest? (BTW—Who would have thought we'd be answering questions like this?!)

How can you use the truths about God from Isaiah 40 to stabilize and strengthen your thinking in the midst of your current circumstances?

Yes, there is more . . .

18 *To whom then will you liken God?*

   Or what likeness will you compare with Him?

19 *As* for *the idol, a craftsman casts it,*

   A goldsmith plates it with gold,

   And a silversmith fashions *chains of silver.*

20 *He who is too impoverished for* such *an offering*

   Selects a tree that does not rot;

   He seeks out for himself a skillful craftsman

   To prepare an idol that will not totter.

21 *Do you not know? Have you not heard?*

Has it not been declared to you from the beginning?

Have you not understood from the foundations of the earth?

A Few More Questions

What do people try and replace God with according to the text? What is the obvious problem?

What kind of idols do we trust in? What things serve as "gods" in the lives of people today? What are the obvious problems with our idols?

Why do you think we gravitate toward idols even when we know better? How can we replace this inclination with truth?

He is truly indescribable. . .

22 *It is He who sits above the circle of the earth,*

And its inhabitants are like grasshoppers,

Who stretches out the heavens like a curtain

And spreads them out like a tent to dwell in.

23 *He* it is *who reduces rulers to nothing,*

Who makes the judges of the earth meaningless.

24 *Scarcely have they been planted,*

Scarcely have they been sown,

Scarcely has their stock taken root in the earth,

But He merely blows on them, and they wither,

And the storm carries them away like stubble.

25 *"To whom then will you liken Me*

That I would be his *equal?" says the Holy One.*

26 *Lift up your eyes on high*

And see who has created these stars,

The One who leads forth their host by number,

He calls them all by name;

Because of the greatness of His might and the strength of His *power,*

Not one of them *is missing.*

27 *Why do you say, O Jacob, and assert, O Israel,*

"My way is hidden from the LORD,

And the justice due me escapes the notice of my God"?

A Few More Questions

How is God described in these verses with reference to the physical earth?

How is He compared to earthly rulers?

What are people called to do in verse 26? Do you pay attention to God's work in this way?

And finally . . .

28　*Do you not know? Have you not heard?*

　　The Everlasting God, the LORD, the Creator of the ends of the earth

　　Does not become weary or tired.

　　His understanding is inscrutable.

29　*He gives strength to the weary,*

　　And to him who *lacks might He increases power.*

30　*Though youths grow weary and tired,*

　　And vigorous young men stumble badly,

31　*Yet those who wait for the LORD*

　　Will gain new strength;

They will mount up with wings like eagles,

They will run and not get tired,

They will walk and not become weary.

Some Final Questions

Do *you* know about God? Have *you* heard about Him? Are you responding to the truth you know and have heard, or are you setting up your own idols?

What does Isaiah remind the people about God? How does this summarize everything that he has been saying throughout the chapter?

Of all the things Isaiah 40 teaches about God, what is the attribute that you most need to be reminded of today? How will you go about remembering it?

Next week we'll consider how we can press into God more through His Word. The better we know Him, the easier it is to trust Him and to wait on Him . . . and the way we get to know Him is through the Word He has revealed to us!

EXTRA

Enjoy these extra opportunities!

Leisure Reading

Keep up your leisure reading! Share with someone else what you've been learning and applying from Scripture.

Intentional Encouragement

Reach out to someone this week and encourage that person in the Lord. Write down who you reached out to and how it was received.

Memorize Key Verses

Pick a key verse or two from Isaiah 40, write it below, and commit it to memory.

#Hashtag It

Make a hashtag for Isaiah 40.

"Post" It

Summarize what you've learned this week in 280 characters or less.

Now take 280 more characters to summarize how you're applying what you've learned!

Lesson Eight

Feeding Yourself

Have you ever fasted? Maybe it was for a blood draw, perhaps it was for Lent, to lose weight, or for some other reason altogether. Maybe you just ended up in the wrong place at the wrong time and had to go without a meal or without several meals. It's not fun. In fact, our culture has coined the word "hangry" to describe the mood that's whipped up when hungry dates angry.

Although we may periodically fast for spiritual or physical reasons, when we consistently go without food for sustained lengths of time we do so at peril to ourselves and to those around us. This is especially true when we forgo the spiritual sustenance of God's Word. Without food and water our physical bodies grow weary and weak within hours. Why do we think we can live strong lives in the Spirit without learning to feed ourselves from God's Word?

For some, sitting down to read the Bible is as natural as breathing. For others it's hard—sometimes *really* hard—but it doesn't have to be. When the Spirit helps us to understand and when we submit to His work in our lives, we can learn to read and to enjoy the Word. In our final two lessons, we'll look at how we can do our part in pursuing God through His Word by the power of His Holy Spirit.

WHERE ARE YOU TODAY?

What challenges do you face in getting into God's Word for yourself?

What successes have you had?

How have others encouraged you in the Word?

How are you encouraging others?

FYI

When You Need a Little Help

Most of what we read in the Bible is clear. Sometimes it's so clear, in fact, that we find it abrasive! LOL! I don't need someone to help me figure out what James is saying about the tongue . . . my problem is living in submission to its truth. There are times, though, when we run into cultural situations and such where we can benefit from a little outside help.

When you've read and studied and are still coming up empty, it's helpful to have a solid Bible commentary on hand. One that I use is *The Moody Bible Commentary*. It is written by conservative Bible scholars, yet easy to understand.

Now having said that, don't get all lazy on me and decide to jump right into a commentary when you first furrow your brow. Commentaries are helpful *after* we've done our own study to help confirm that we are on the right track or to help correct us if we've veered from the text. Generally, you'll find that when you study diligently on your own, you'll come to the same conclusions as the commentators!

THE EPISODE VERSUS THE SERIES

Sometimes our core problem with getting into the Word of God is that we're having a hard time understanding the section we're looking at. We simply don't understand the scene that's right in front of us, the psalm, the proverb, etc. Other times, though, it's because we don't understand how the "episode," so to speak, fits into the "series"—how the part of the Bible we're reading fits into the Bible as a whole. Let me explain.

As we walk through life, we often come into the middle of stories. It happens every time we meet a new person and we start getting to know them. We learn of their history, their backstory over time. It happens when we read books, watch television, or go to the movies. Our entertainment industry is built on multiple-season stories and multiple-film epics complete with backstory flashbacks and overarching storylines that require attention to detail over time. We love it in our entertainment, we typically enjoy it in our relationships, but often we view similar complexity frustrating in God's Word.

Full disclosure here: I used to find this overwhelming, too! I wanted to know everything I could about God's Word . . . *now!* As I've gotten older, though, I'm learning to appreciate the truth that I will never *run out* of God's Word regardless of how many times I read it. There is no situation in life to which I will not be able to apply it, and I can study and study and study and I will never be able to exhaust it! I hope you'll learn to let that encourage rather than discourage you, and that you'll let it spur you on to more and deeper study!

As we learn to handle the Word for ourselves, to take in what we need to grow, we'll need to learn how to pay attention to the "episodes" *and* to start understanding how they fit into the "series" as a whole! Of course it's easier to do this with some texts than with others, but when we start with the understanding that Scripture as a whole points to the Gospel—God's saving work in Jesus Christ at the cross—we're well on our way to fitting the pieces together!

Today, we're going to work through a text that's pretty clear—the four-chapter book of Ruth. We'll start by summarizing the very basics of what the episode is about and then we'll do a little more work at uncovering how it fits into the bigger picture.

LET'S READ

Grab a Bible or open one on your tablet and turn to the book of Ruth. Take about 15 minutes to read through this concise 4-chapter book in one sitting. When you're done, we'll practice asking the 5 W and H questions as they pertain to this "episode" and then as they pertain to the "series."

Let's Ask Some Questions—The Episode

Summarize Ruth's immediate-context story, making sure to address the questions *Who? What? When? Where? Why?* and *How?* Simply put: How would you explain this short story to someone else?

Asking these basic questions and follow-ups is a simple tool to use both when looking at the immediate context of a book and the greater context of Scripture as a whole. Even if it seems unnatural at first, it will become second nature soon enough! Just keep at it!

Let's Ask Some Questions—The Series

As we ask these questions, we'll be seeking to address how Ruth fits into the greater storyline of Scripture.

Ruth 1

When do the events in the book of Ruth occur relative to the rest of the biblical narrative?

When did the judges rule?

As we've already seen, the book of Ruth takes place "when the judges governed" (Ruth 1:1). This puts it in a very specific place in the biblical text—after the time of Moses and Joshua and prior to the time of the kings of Israel and Judah.

What significance does the town of Bethlehem have in Scripture? (Not sure? See Micah 5:2 and Matthew 2:1-12.)

How does the country of Moab fit in? What beliefs did its people hold? There are plenty of answers right in the text of Ruth. If you use other biblical sources, jot down your references.

What did you learn about Ruth and Naomi?

What does this chapter teach about God?

What was the time of the judges like?
The time of the judges was a lot like today. People did what they wanted to do, regardless of God's command. Account after account illustrates the continual cycles of disobedience, defeat, and God's eventual deliverance when the people cry out to Him. Here is how the book of Judges summaries it:

"In those days there was no king in Israel; everyone did what was right in his own eyes" (Judges 21:25).

How do the characters in this chapter view God?

Ruth 2

Describe Boaz from the text.

Based on this text, what role does the extended family play in Israel?

How did those with little or no money (including foreigners) subsist in ancient Israel?

How do Ruth and Boaz meet? Do you think it is coincidence or something more? Explain your answer.

How does Boaz view Ruth's relationship to the God of Israel? What does he specifically say in Ruth 2:12? Where has Ruth sought refuge?

What does Ruth 2 teach about God?

Ruth 3

How does Naomi set out to take care of Ruth in chapter 3? What instructions does she give her?

What's your reaction to this? On first hearing it? On second read? Write down your thoughts and/or questions.

What do we already know about Boaz from the text?

What about Ruth?

What practical problem does Ruth need help with? (See 3:13.)

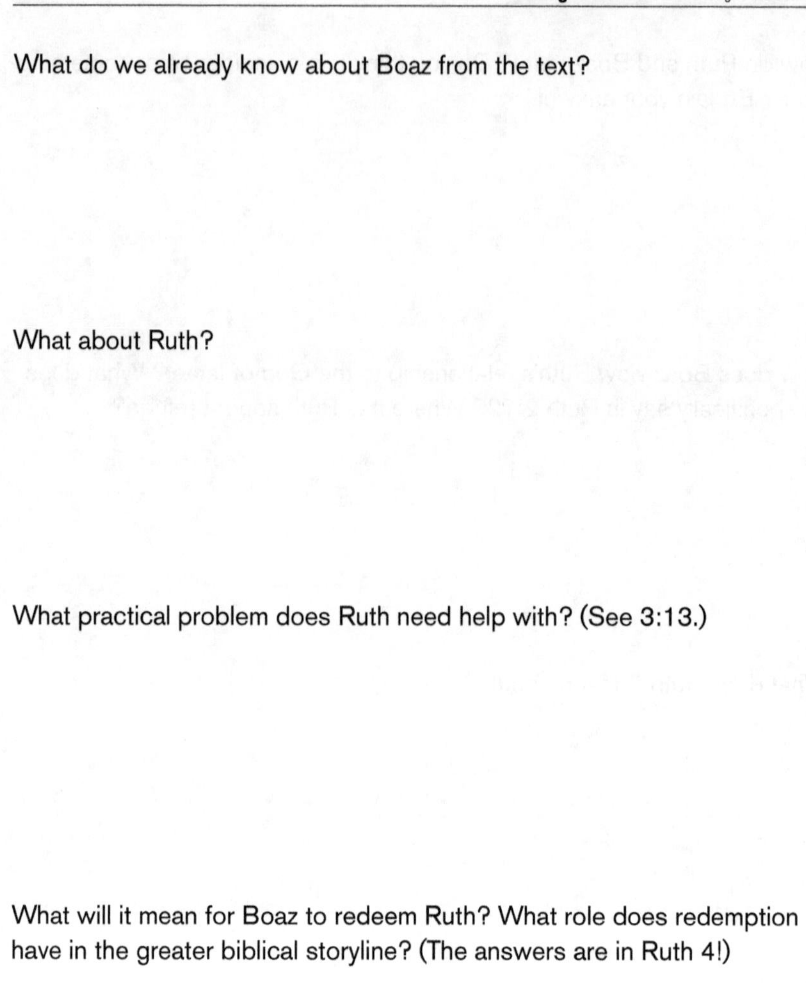

What will it mean for Boaz to redeem Ruth? What role does redemption have in the greater biblical storyline? (The answers are in Ruth 4!)

Ruth 4

How and why do Ruth and Boaz end up married? Does Boaz have to marry Ruth? Explain.

Who are Rachel and Leah, and what do they have to do with Ruth? (See Genesis 29–30.)

What difference does a redeemer make in Ruth's life?

Let's Mark

Before we call it a day, let's see how Ruth fits into the greater narrative of Scripture by checking out Matthew 1. As you read, simply mark references to anyone you know!

Matthew 1:1-17

1 *The record of the genealogy of Jesus the Messiah, the son of David, the son of Abraham:*

2 *Abraham was the father of Isaac, Isaac the father of Jacob, and Jacob the father of Judah and his brothers.*

3 *Judah was the father of Perez and Zerah by Tamar, Perez was the father of Hezron, and Hezron the father of Ram.*

4 *Ram was the father of Amminadab, Amminadab the father of Nahshon, and Nahshon the father of Salmon.*

5 *Salmon was the father of Boaz by Rahab, Boaz was the father of Obed by Ruth, and Obed the father of Jesse.*

6	*Jesse was the father of David the king.*

David was the father of Solomon by Bathsheba who had been the wife of Uriah.

7	*Solomon was the father of Rehoboam, Rehoboam the father of Abijah, and Abijah the father of Asa.*

8	*Asa was the father of Jehoshaphat, Jehoshaphat the father of Joram, and Joram the father of Uzziah.*

9	*Uzziah was the father of Jotham, Jotham the father of Ahaz, and Ahaz the father of Hezekiah.*

10	*Hezekiah was the father of Manasseh, Manasseh the father of Amon, and Amon the father of Josiah.*

11	*Josiah became the father of Jeconiah and his brothers, at the time of the deportation to Babylon.*

12	*After the deportation to Babylon: Jeconiah became the father of Shealtiel, and Shealtiel the father of Zerubbabel.*

13	*Zerubbabel was the father of Abihud, Abihud the father of Eliakim, and Eliakim the father of Azor.*

14	*Azor was the father of Zadok, Zadok the father of Achim, and Achim the father of Eliud.*

15	*Eliud was the father of Eleazar, Eleazar the father of Matthan, and Matthan the father of Jacob.*

16	*Jacob was the father of Joseph the husband of Mary, by whom Jesus was born, who is called the Messiah.*

17 So all the generations from Abraham to David are fourteen generations; from David to the deportation to Babylon, fourteen generations; and from the deportation to Babylon to the Messiah, fourteen generations.

Final Questions for the Week . . .

Who did you recognize in Matthew 1 from reading and studying Ruth? How are all of these folks connected to Jesus?

What additional information does Matthew tell us about Boaz's mother? Did this one surprise you?! (If you want to learn more about Boaz's mom, her story shows up in Joshua 2 and Joshua 6.) Are you beginning to see how it all fits together?!

How would you explain Ruth's relationship to the redemption story running through Scripture? What do we learn about redemption?

What do we learn about God? What do we learn about God seeking and saving Gentiles even in the Old Testament?

What better and more complete Redeemer does God's Word tell us about, and what difference is this Redeemer making in your life? (See Galatians 4:4-6, Titus 2:11-14, 1 Peter 1:17-19.)

See, it's not that hard . . . but at the same time, there are some fun and challenging puzzles to explore! As you finish today, spend some time asking God to help you see if there is anything holding you back from pursuing Him zealously through His Word. Then jot down below any encumbrances that He brings to mind.

EXTRA

Let this section encourage you and spur you on to enjoy the Word of God!

Leisure Reading

Keep up your leisure Bible reading! Share with someone else what you've been learning and applying.

Intentional Encouragement

Reach out to someone this week and encourage that person in the Lord. Write down who you reached out to and how it was received.

Memorize Key Verses

Looking to memorize something from Ruth this week? Why not commit to heart Ruth 2:12 . . .

"May the LORD reward your work, and your wages be full from the LORD, the God of Israel, under whose wings you have come to seek refuge."

#Hashtag It

Make a hashtag for Ruth by chapter and for the book as a whole.

Ruth 1

Ruth 2

Ruth 3

Ruth 4

The Book of Ruth

"Post" It

Summarize what you've learned this week in 280 characters or less.

Now summarize how you're applying what you've learned this week in 280 characters or less!

Lesson Nine
Encouraging Others and Running Light

"And Jonathan, Saul's son, arose and went to David at Horesh, and encouraged him in God."
—1 Samuel 23:16

When the days grow dark and long, when lawlessness increases and opposition abounds we need to strengthen ourselves in the Lord *and* we need to encourage others! We've already seen from Isaiah the need to strengthen ourselves by waiting on the Lord and pursuing Him through His Word, but God has not put us on the planet alone. None of us is an island. When we belong to Christ, we are part of His body, His building, His bride. In short, when we are in Him, we are part of each other and we have a responsibility to encourage each other and to help one another grow.

IS YOUR WEARINESS WANING?

There is no quick fix for weariness. Still, as we walk with God in His Word, as we wait on Him, as we follow His ways and throw off encumbrances and weights we were never intended to carry, we begin to notice our strength being renewed. We begin to realize we are walking in His power and relying on the working of His Holy Spirit within us instead of soldiering through on our own.

So, nine lessons in, is it getting any better? Are you starting to see truths from God's Word that are helping you to walk more and more according to God's life-giving truth?

WHERE ARE YOU TODAY?

Has your weariness level changed over the past couple of months? What, if anything, has improved? What, if anything, has gotten worse? Why do you think this is?

Has how you deal with weariness changed at all? If so, how and why?

Has your view of weariness changed? How do you view it now compared to when you started this study?

What truths from God's Word have been the most helpful in your battle against growing weary and losing heart? Write them down below along with how you're applying them.

ENCOURAGING ONE ANOTHER

When we read the Psalms, it becomes clear that David and the other psalmists knew how to strengthen and encourage themselves in the Lord. In psalm after psalm we read of David recounting terrible and frightening circumstances with enemies on every side but then reminding himself about the Lord and casting himself on His sovereign God who saves.

David knew God. David followed God. Still, when the going got rough, David's best friend Jonathan risked his own life to seek David out and encourage him in God.

LET'S EXPLORE!

To set the context for the verses we'll be looking at, read 1 Samuel 23 in your Bible. As you do, remember that Saul is hunting David and intending to kill him. In going out to encourage David, Jonathan is actively opposing his murderous father.

Let's Start by Marking

So we don't miss anything about Jonathan, let's mark:

- references to Jonathan
- references to Jonathan's actions

1 Samuel 23:16-17

16 And Jonathan, Saul's son, arose and went to David at Horesh, and encouraged him in God.

17 Thus he said to him, "Do not be afraid, because the hand of Saul my father will not find you, and you will be king over Israel and I will be next to you; and Saul my father knows that also."

A Few Questions

(Based on **1 Samuel 23**)

How do you think Saul would have responded if he knew Jonathan was sneaking out to encourage David? (Not sure? Check out 1 Samuel 20, also.)

What was involved in Jonathan encouraging David in God? (Watch the verbs as you answer.)

What effort do you expend in encouraging others in God? What are ways you can (or already do!) intentionally encourage others in the Lord?

What simple ways of encouragement are in your path every day?

How, specifically, did Jonathan encourage David in God? What was the content of the encouragement?

What can you learn from this with regard to encouraging others?

LET'S EXPLORE!

As we near the end of our time, let's look at three short excerpts from the letter to the Hebrews specifically with reference to encouraging one another. The first two address the why and the how of encouraging one another in the Lord. The final one is the text of Scripture that has encouraged me in the Lord as much as any ever has, and so it is one of the texts I want to leave with you as we near the finish line.

Let's Start by Marking

This time around, let's mark:

- references to encourage/encouraging
- references to any acts of encouragement you notice

Hebrews 3:12-13

In Hebrews 3, the letter's author asserts that Jesus is better than Moses and warns the Hebrews not to walk the way of the Exodus generation whose hardened hearts rebelled against God.

12 *Take care, brethren, that there not be in any one of you an evil, unbelieving heart that falls away from the living God.*

13 *But encourage one another day after day, as long as it is still called "Today," so that none of you will be hardened by the deceitfulness of sin.*

A Few Questions . . .

What warning precedes the exhortation to "encourage"?

How does encouraging one another help believers to hold fast?

How often are believers to encourage each other? Why? How are you at doing this?

What threat does sin pose according to verse 13? Do you think this danger has increased at all during your lifetime? Explain.

How can you encourage others? How are you encouraged by others?

Hebrews 10:19-25

Hebrews 10 portrays Christ as "the one sacrifice for sins for all time" (Hebrews 10:12), the only perfect sacrifice. In verses 19-25, the author of Hebrews calls his readers to live in the light of this.

19 *Therefore, brethren, since we have confidence to enter the holy place by the blood of Jesus,*

20 *by a new and living way which He inaugurated for us through the veil, that is, His flesh,*

21 *and since we have a great priest over the house of God,*

22 *let us draw near with a sincere heart in full assurance of faith, having our hearts sprinkled clean from an evil conscience and our bodies washed with pure water.*

23 *Let us hold fast the confession of our hope without wavering, for He who promised is faithful;*

24 *and let us consider how to stimulate one another to love and good deeds,*

25 *not forsaking our own assembling together, as is the habit of some, but encouraging one another; and all the more as you see the day drawing near.*

A Few Questions . . .

What exhortations does the author of Hebrews make in these verses? We can find them by looking for the "Let us . . ." phrases.

Which of the exhortations are focused on our relationship with God?

Based on what we've learned so far from the Word, what are some ways we can draw near and hold fast?

What exhortations focus on our behavior toward and with others? How are you doing at these?

What specifically are we not to forsake? Are you ever prone to this? If so, when and why? How can you combat this?

What should spur us on to further encouraging one another?

Who, specifically, *will* you encourage today?

Let's Mark

Hebrews 11 recounts the lives of people who lived by faith in the one true God. If you have time, it would be great for you to read the whole chapter before we look at Hebrews 12:1-3! Then let's mark:

- the exhortations (look for "let us" and what follows)
- *grow weary* and *lose heart*

Hebrews 12:1-3

1 *Therefore, since we have so great a cloud of witnesses surrounding us, let us also lay aside every encumbrance and the sin which so easily entangles us, and let us run with endurance the race that is set before us,*

2 *fixing our eyes on Jesus, the author and perfecter of faith, who for the joy set before Him endured the cross, despising the shame, and has sat down at the right hand of the throne of God.*

3 *For consider Him who has endured such hostility by sinners against Himself, so that you will not grow weary and lose heart.*

A Few Questions . . .

Who is the great cloud of witnesses? What are these people known for?

What does the author of Hebrews call his readers to lay aside? How are these similar? How do they differ?

Do you think it is possible for a good thing to be an encumbrance? If so, how?

Are there any "good things" that encumber you? What are they?

How can good things contribute to weariness?

If you need to lay down a "good" encumbrance, spend some time prayerfully considering your exit strategy.

What about sins? Are you entangled in anything you need God to free you from? If so, write it down, confess it before God, and ask Him to help you walk in freedom.

What positive actions are we to take once we're unencumbered?

How are you going to fix your eyes on Jesus and start running more unencumbered this week?

According to verse 3, how can considering Jesus, that is thinking carefully about Him, help us as we run our race?

What's Your Next Step?

It would be easy to set this study down and move on and away quietly. My prayer is that you won't. My prayer is that you will not only consider what encumbrances are hanging around your life and what barriers are impeding your way into the Word, but that you will take steps to throw them off and dismantle them. We will be spiritually weary if we are not pursuing God through His Word. It's that simple. If you don't eat, you grow weak. If you don't consider Jesus, it is easy to grow weary and lose heart.

What will it take to ensure that you are prioritizing your time with God? Only you can answer that question. Will you? Will you act on it? If so, take a few minutes to write down your next steps below and prayerfully ask God to give you the strength to carry them through!

My next steps . . .

Digging Deeper

Don't Weary When God Trains You

The author of Hebrews reminds his readers not to faint under the Lord's discipline (from the Greek: *paideuo,* a word used for the formation and training of a child). If you have some extra time, dive into Hebrews 12:4-13.

Here are some questions to consider:

Who does God discipline and why? (v. 7)

What is the purpose, and what does it compare to? (v. 10)

What does it feel like, yet what does it yield? (v. 11)

Given these truths, how are we to respond?

LET'S EXPLORE!

Let us always remember that Jesus' yoke is easy and His burden is light (Matthew 11:28-30). So before we close, let's look at these verses as a reminder, a summary, and a commissioning of sorts for living a life that waits on God. In Matthew 11, Jesus has been teaching in the cities of Israel—likely in the region of Galilee—and has just denounced those that have not repented after witnessing miracles. Still He offers hope!

Let's Start by Marking

This time around, let's mark:

- references to the Father and to the Son
- actions Jesus calls for (beginning in verse 28)

Matthew 11:25-30

25 At that time Jesus said, "I praise You, Father, Lord of heaven

and earth, that You have hidden these things from the wise and

intelligent and have revealed them to infants.

26 "Yes, Father, for this way was well-pleasing in Your sight.

27 "All things have been handed over to Me by My Father; and no one

knows the Son except the Father; nor does anyone know the Father

except the Son, and anyone to whom the Son wills to reveal Him.

28 "Come to Me, all who are weary and heavy-laden, and I will give

you rest.

29 "Take My yoke upon you and learn from Me, for I am gentle and

humble in heart, and YOU WILL FIND REST FOR YOUR SOULS.

30 "For My yoke is easy and My burden is light."

Yoked to Jesus and Not to the Law

A yoke joined two animals together so they could pull a device. While the Jewish people found themselves unable to bear the yoke of the Law, Jesus tells His followers that His yoke is light. When we come to Jesus, we are yoked to Him and His Spirit empowers us to live!

A Few Questions . . .

Who is Jesus speaking to in verses 25-26?

What does Jesus say about the Father in verses 25-27?

Thinking back to Isaiah 40:31 where we learned that "those who wait for the LORD will gain new strength," according to Jesus how can we know the One we are to wait on?

Who is Jesus speaking to in verses 28-30? What is their condition? What do they need?

Can you relate to this? When have you had this need?

How does Jesus call the weary and heavy-laden to respond to Him?

What will Jesus do for those who come to Him? What is specifically stated? What is implied?

What potential dangers do weary and burdened people face if they put their trust in a wrong person? By contrast, how does Jesus describe Himself?

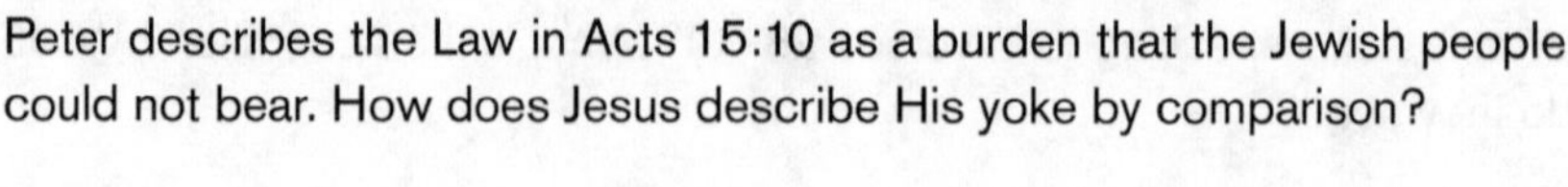

Peter describes the Law in Acts 15:10 as a burden that the Jewish people could not bear. How does Jesus describe His yoke by comparison?

What do people who are yoked to Jesus gain? What process will they undergo?

What will you find?

What are you waiting for?!

While the world wearies itself seeking true soul rest, we as believers do not need to wear ourselves out seeking God's favor or salvation—Jesus has accomplished the hard work that only He can do! In Him we have the soul rest that the whole world seeks in so many varied and destructive ways. Let us declare that truth to those who need Jesus, let us feed on the truth of His Word daily and meditate on His precepts to strengthen us for the path, and let us trust Him to do the work that only He can do in and through us!

EXTRA

Enjoy these extra opportunities!

Leisure Reading

Keep up your leisure reading! Share with someone else what you've been learning and applying from God's Word.

Intentional Encouragement

Reach out to someone this week and encourage that person in the Lord. Write down who you reached out to and how it was received.

Memorize Key Verses

What is your key verse from what you've studied?

#Hashtag It

Make a hashtag for the key truths you've learned during our time in the Word together.

"Post" It

Summarize what you've learned during our study in 280 characters or less.

Now take 280 more characters to summarize how you're applying what you've learned!

Resources

Helpful Study Tools

How to Study Your Bible
Eugene, Oregon: Harvest House
Publishers

The New Inductive Study Bible
Eugene, Oregon: Harvest House
Publishers

Logos Bible Software
Available at www.logos.com.

Greek Word Study Tools

Kittel, G., Friedrich, G., &
Bromiley, G.W.
*Theological Dictionary of the New
Testament, Abridged* (also known
as Little Kittel)
Grand Rapids, Michigan: W.B.
Eerdmans Publishing Company

Hebrew Word Study Tools

Harris, R.L., Archer, G.L., &
Walker, B.K.
*Theological Wordbook of the Old
Testament* (also known as TWOT)
Chicago, Illinois: Moody Press

General Word Study Tools

Strong, James
*The New Strong's Exhaustive
Concordance of the Bible*
Nashville, Tennessee: Thomas
Nelson

Recommended Commentary Sets

Expositor's Bible Commentary
Grand Rapids, Michigan:
Zondervan

NIV Application Commentary
Grand Rapids, Michigan:
Zondervan

The New American Commentary
Nashville, Tennessee: Broadman
and Holman Publishers

One-Volume Commentary

Carson, D.A., France, R.T.,
Motyer, J.A., & Wenham, G.J.,
eds.
*New Bible Commentary: 21st
Century Edition*
Downers Grove, Illinois: Inter-
Varsity Press

Rydelnik, M., Vanlaningham, M.,
eds.
The Moody Bible Commentary
Chicago, Illinois: Moody
Publishers

We'd love to hear from you!

If you found this study helpful, please take

a moment to share your thoughts.

Leave a Review

https://www.pamgillaspieshop.com/products/strength-renewed-learning-to-wait-on-god

OR

Take a Short Survey

https://bit.ly/StrengthRenewedBookSurvey